Mandala
Coloring
Book

Alcohol Markers
coloring book
serie

Scan Me

This Book Belongs To

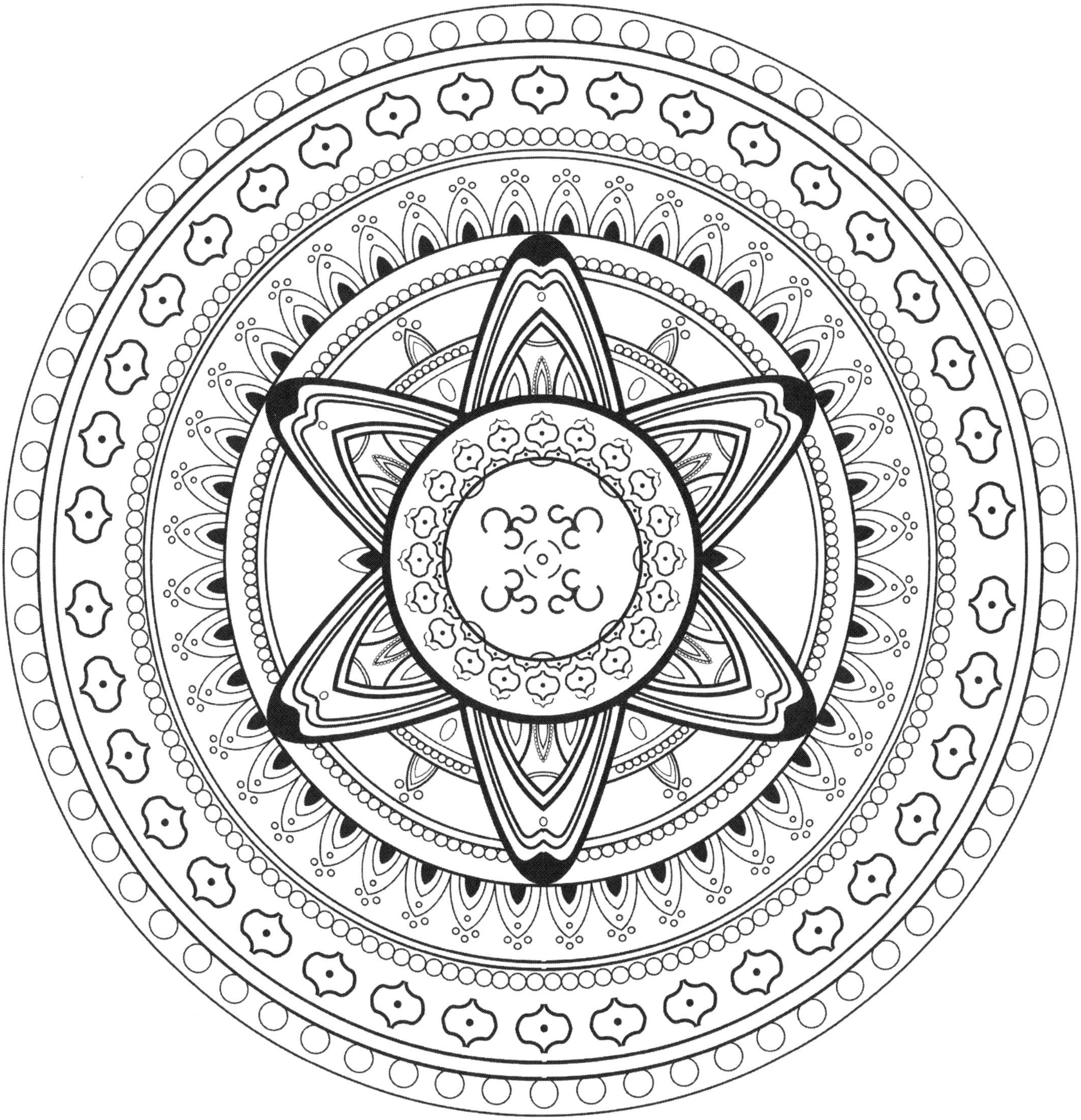

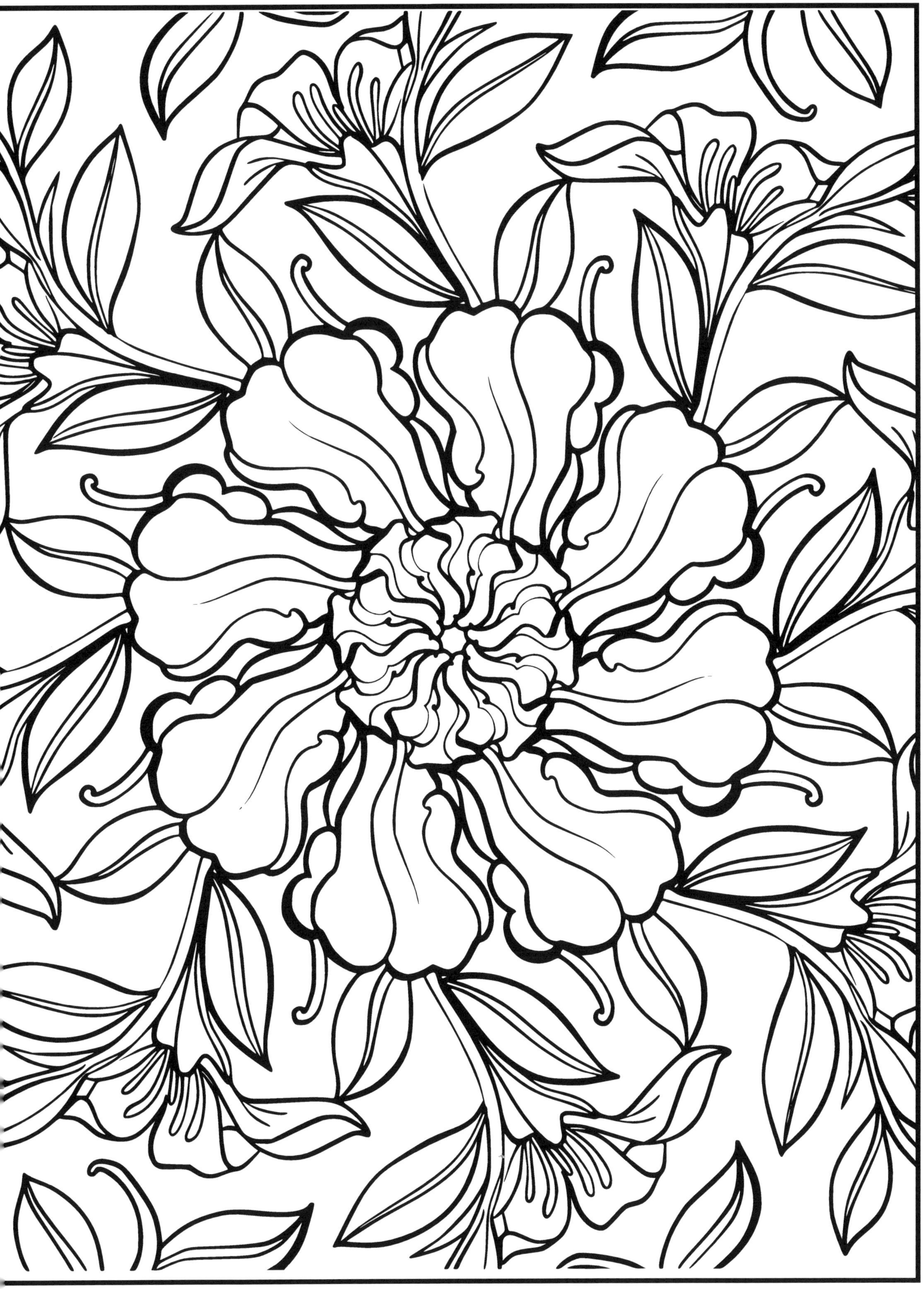

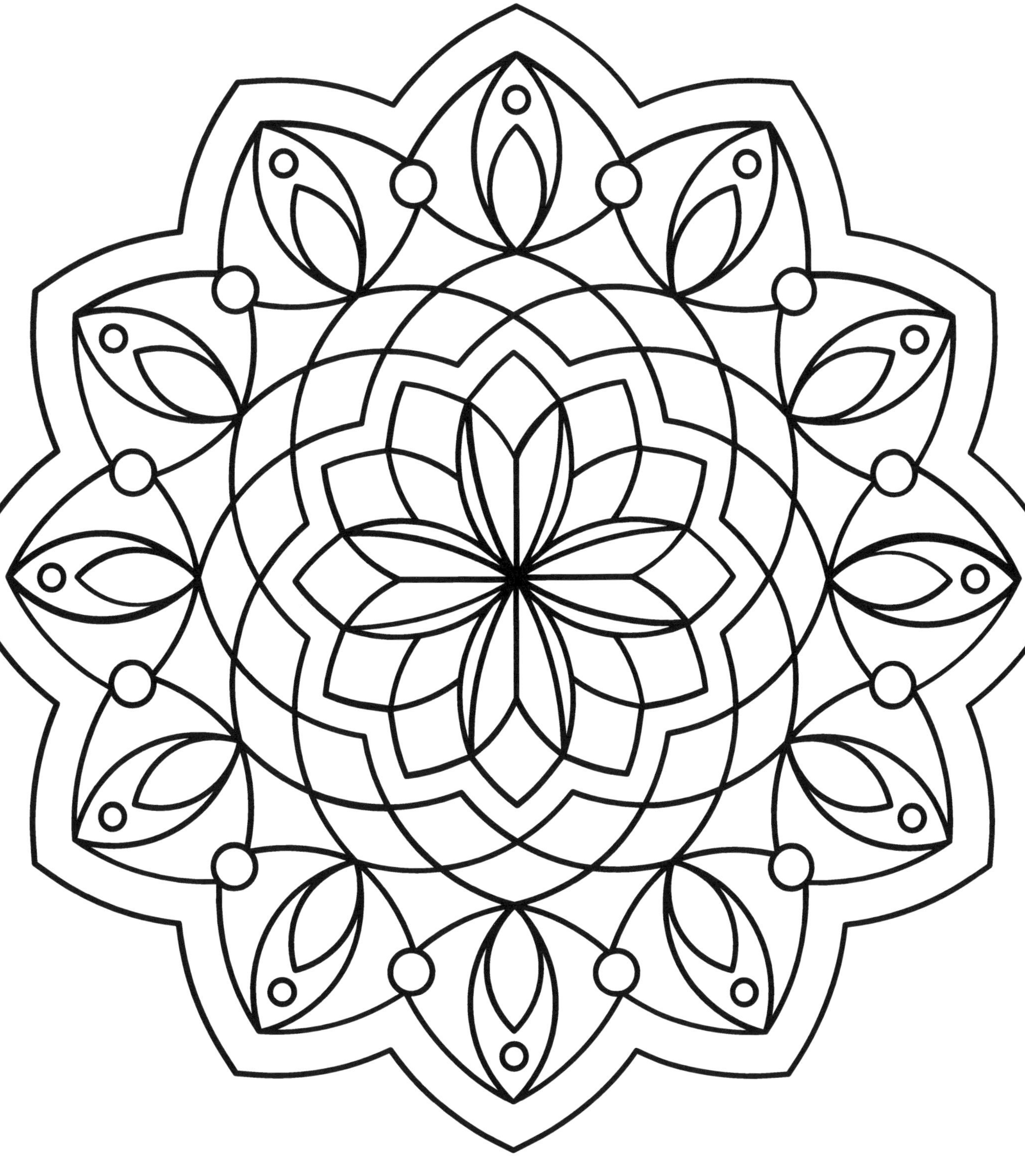

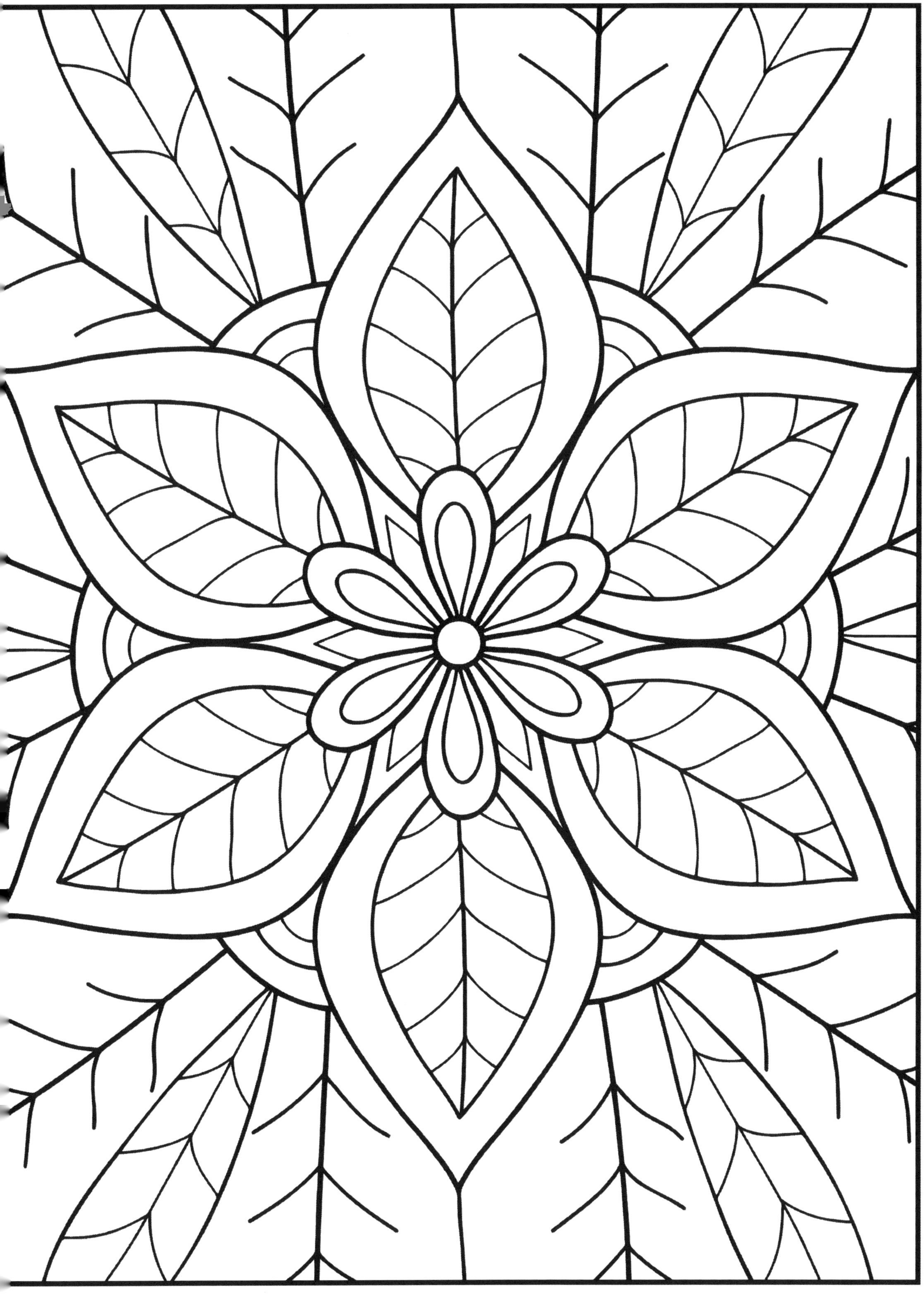

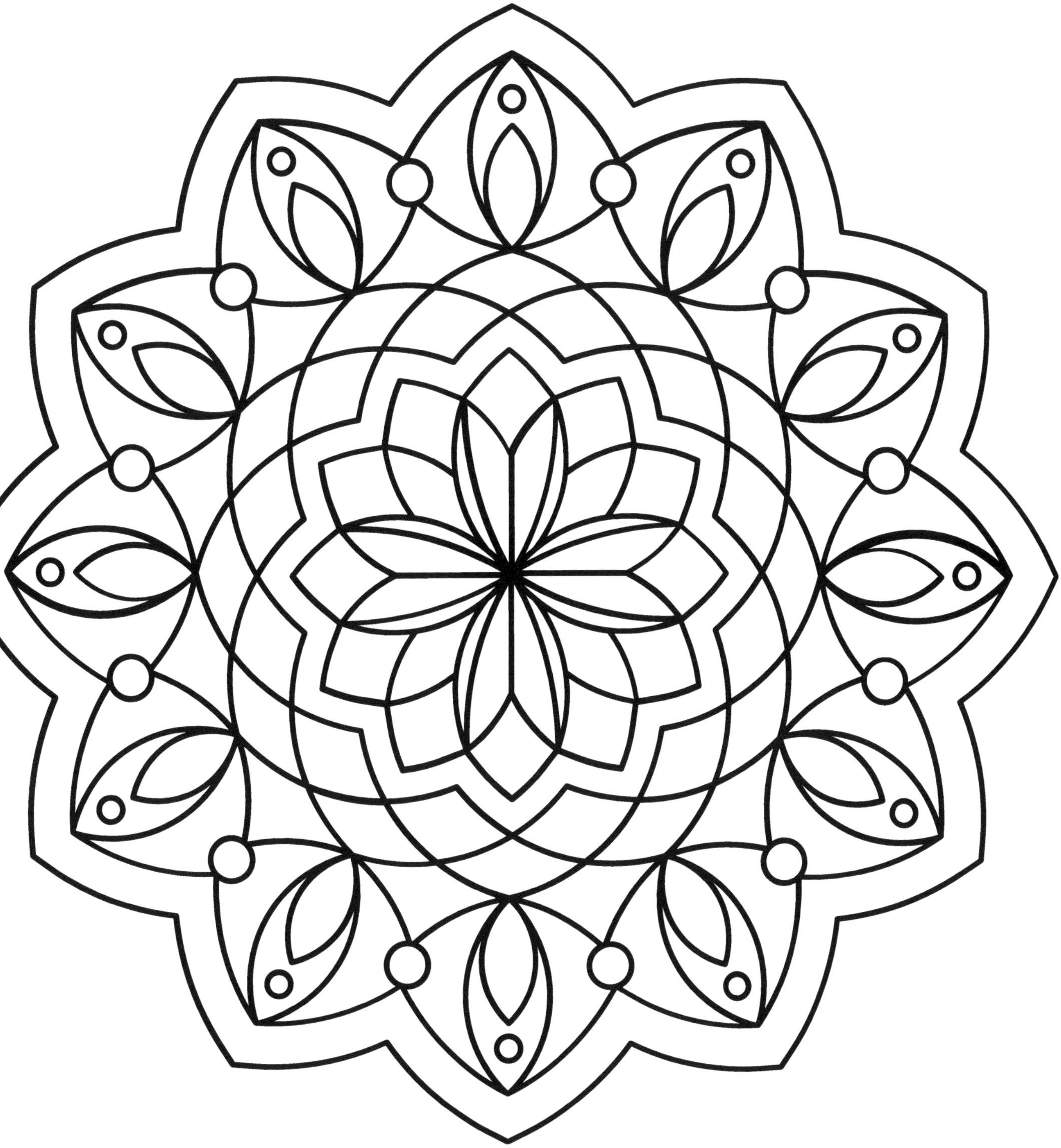

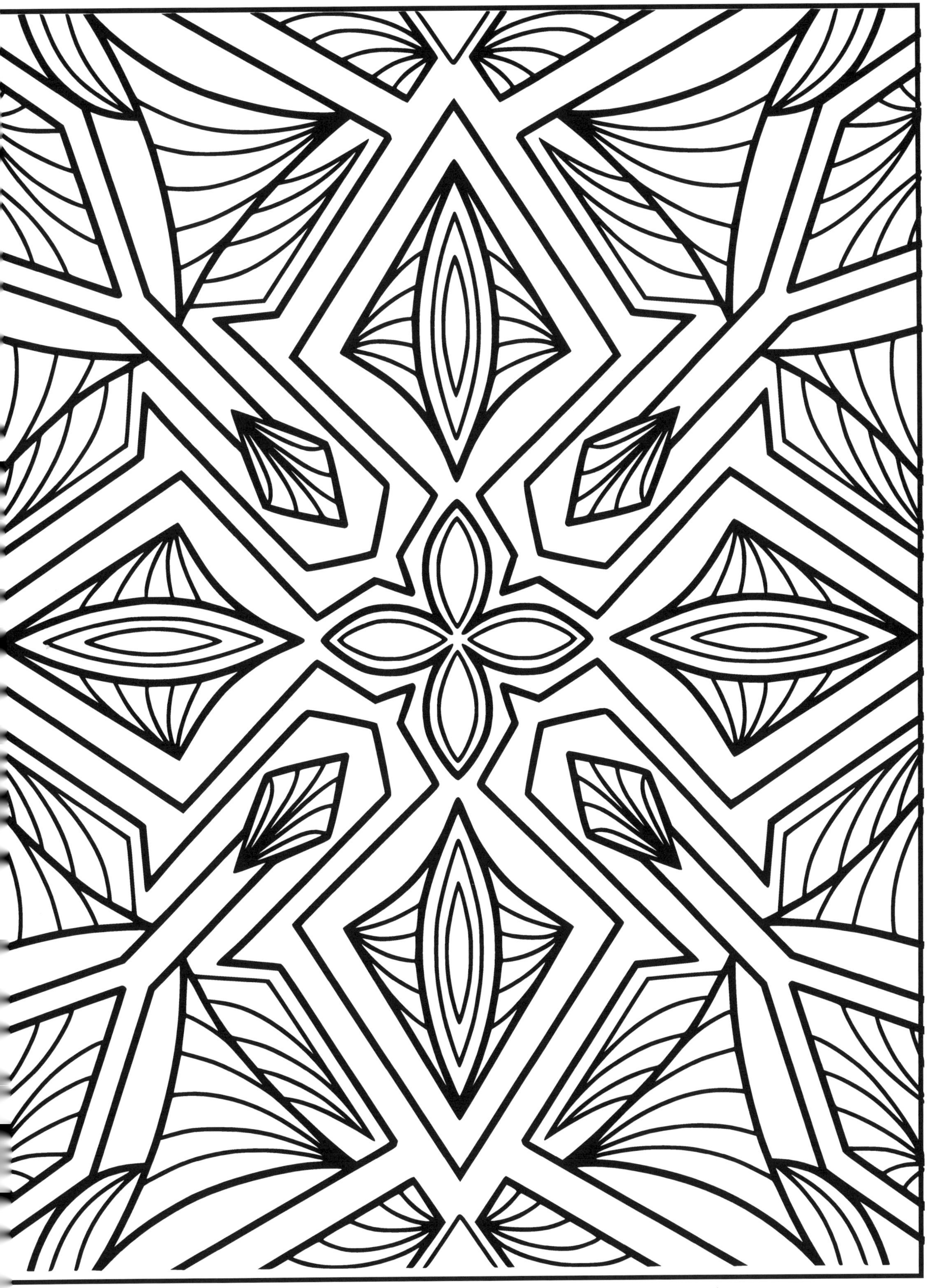

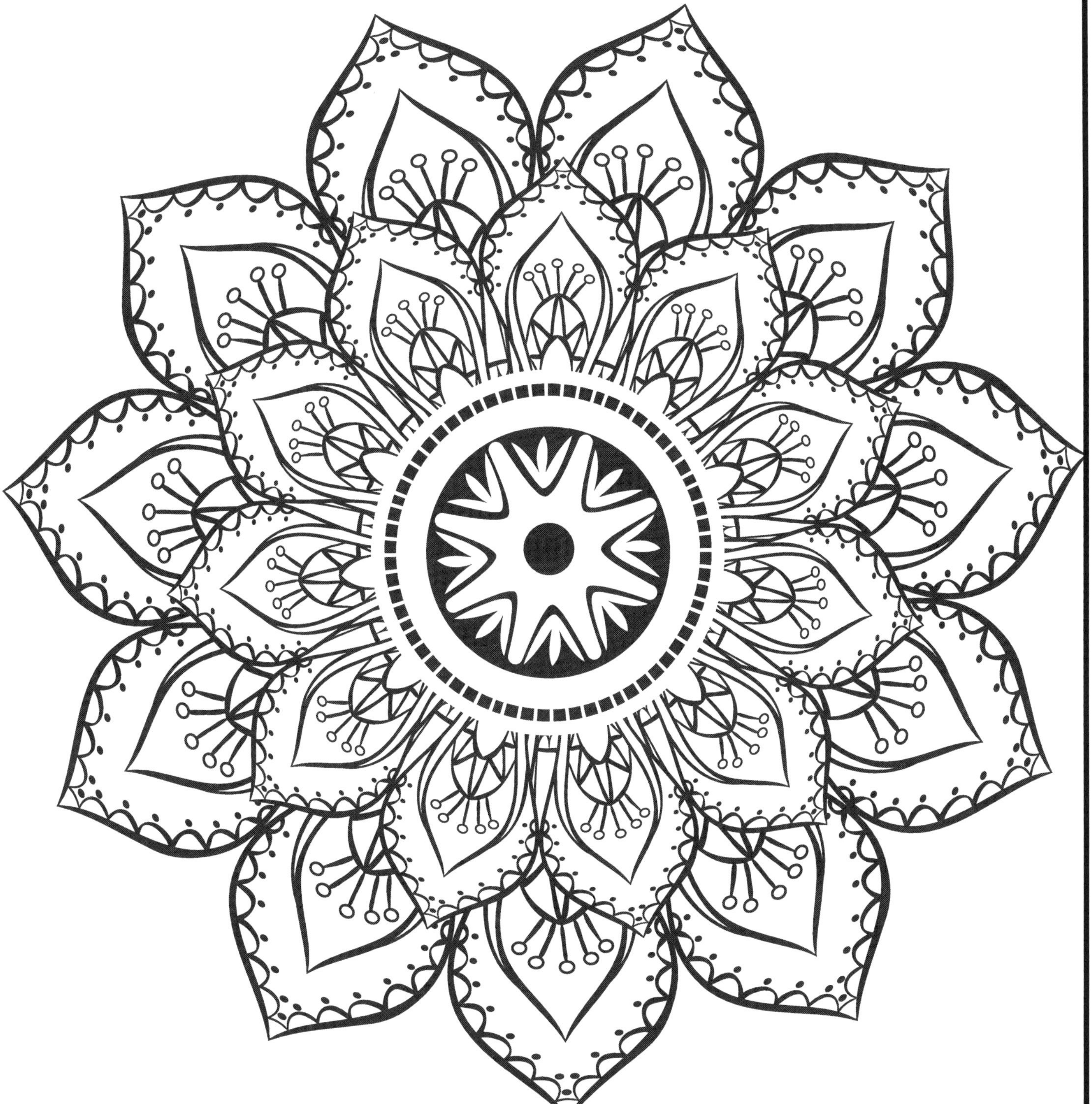

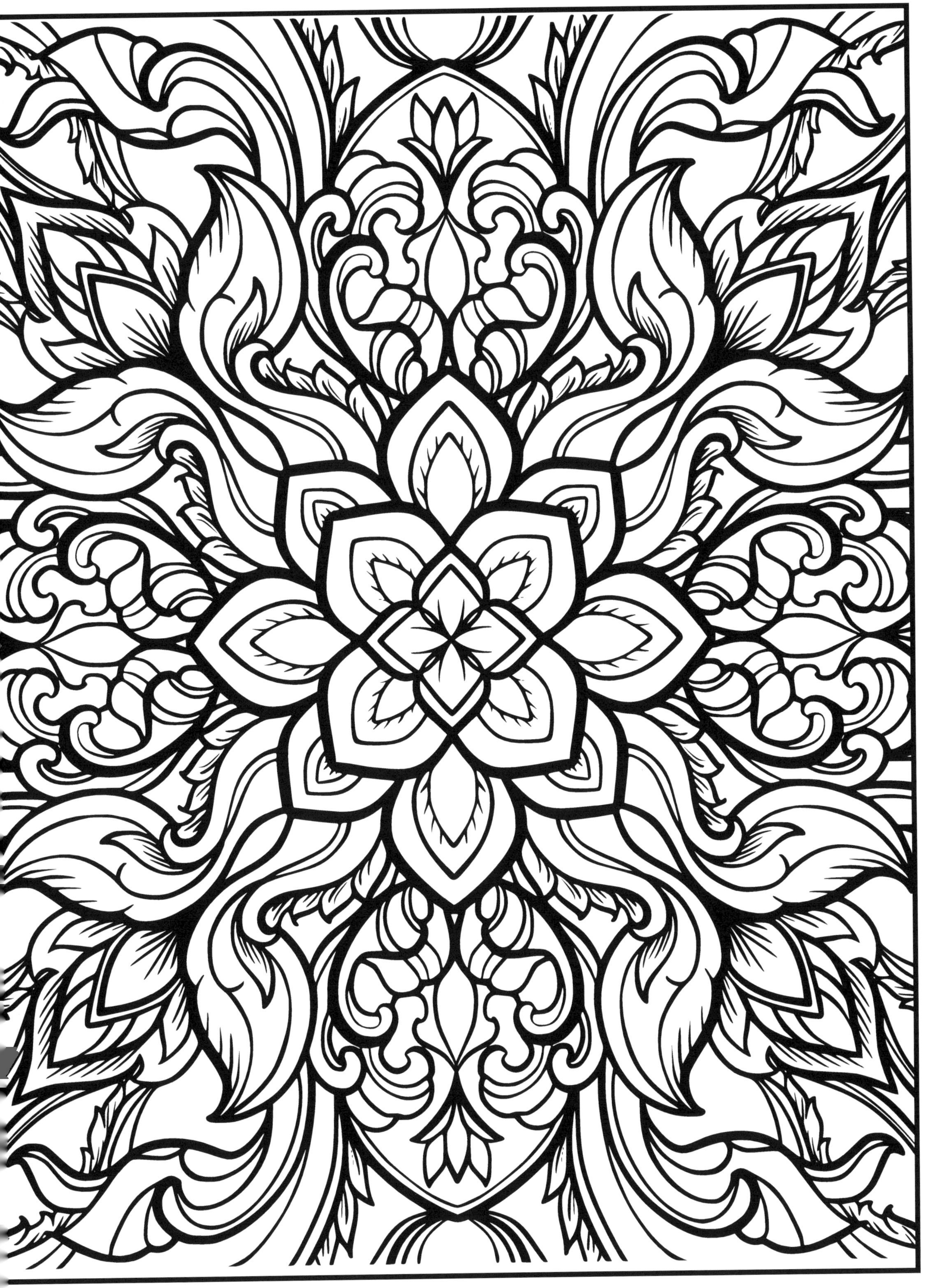

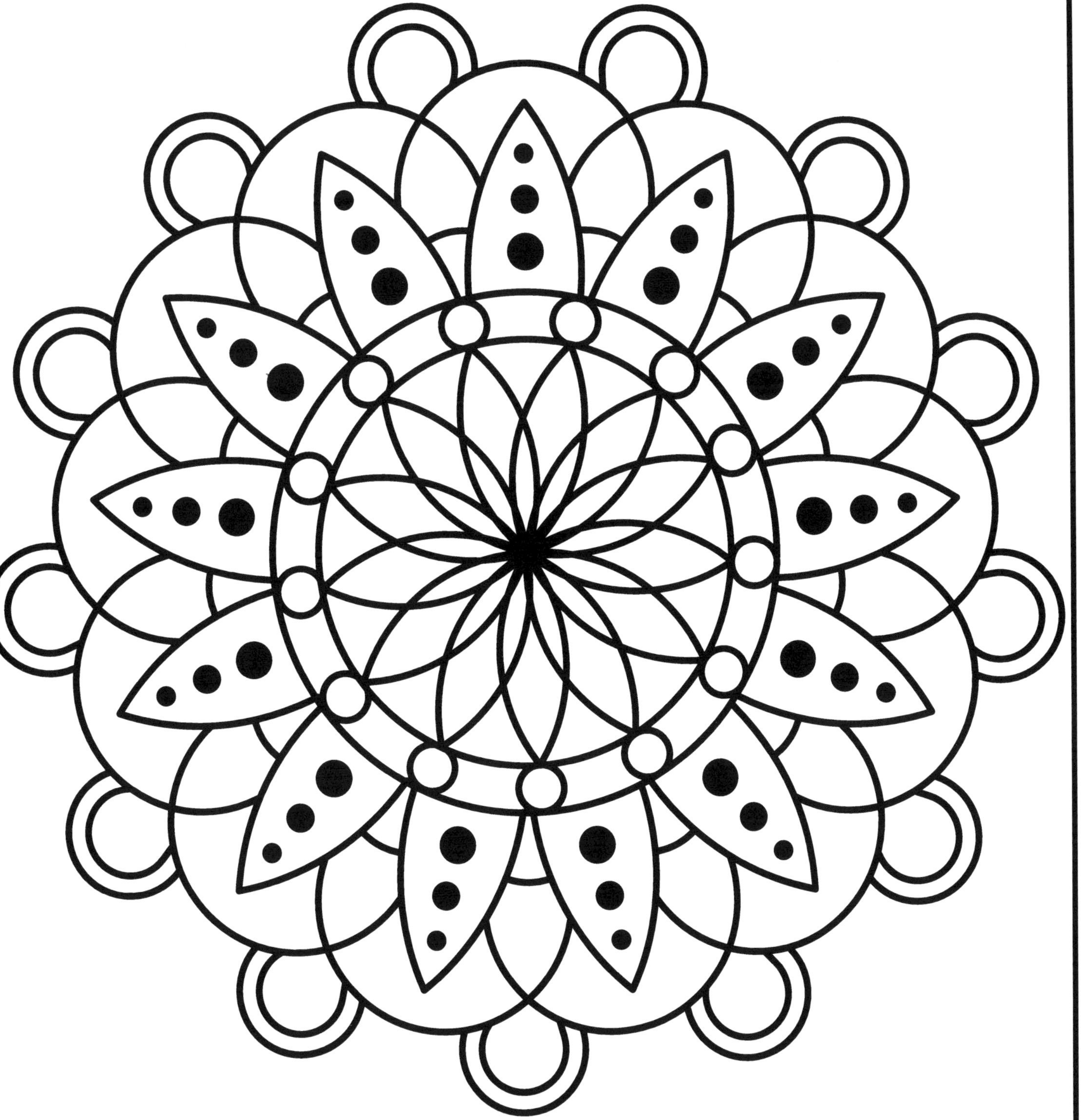

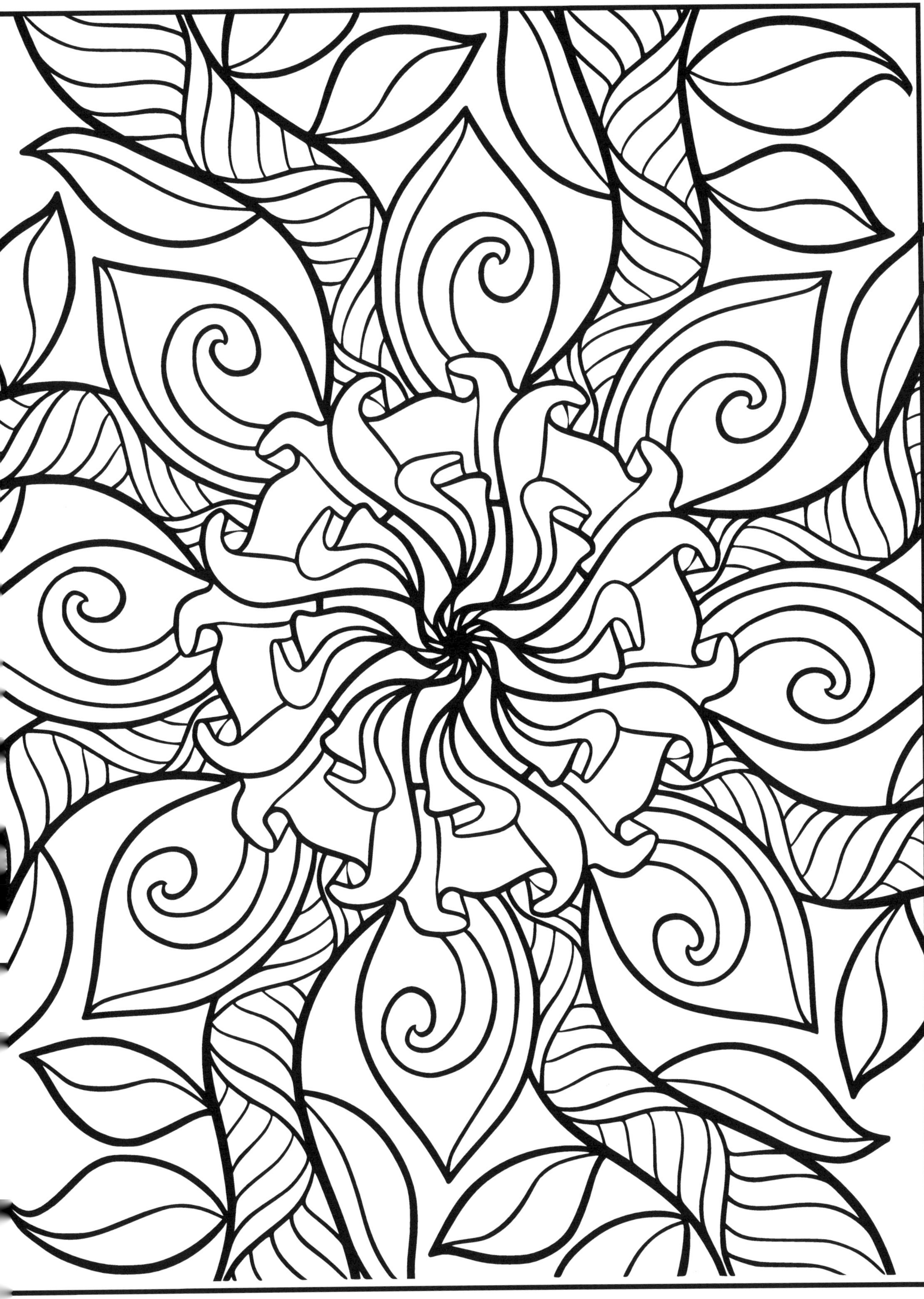

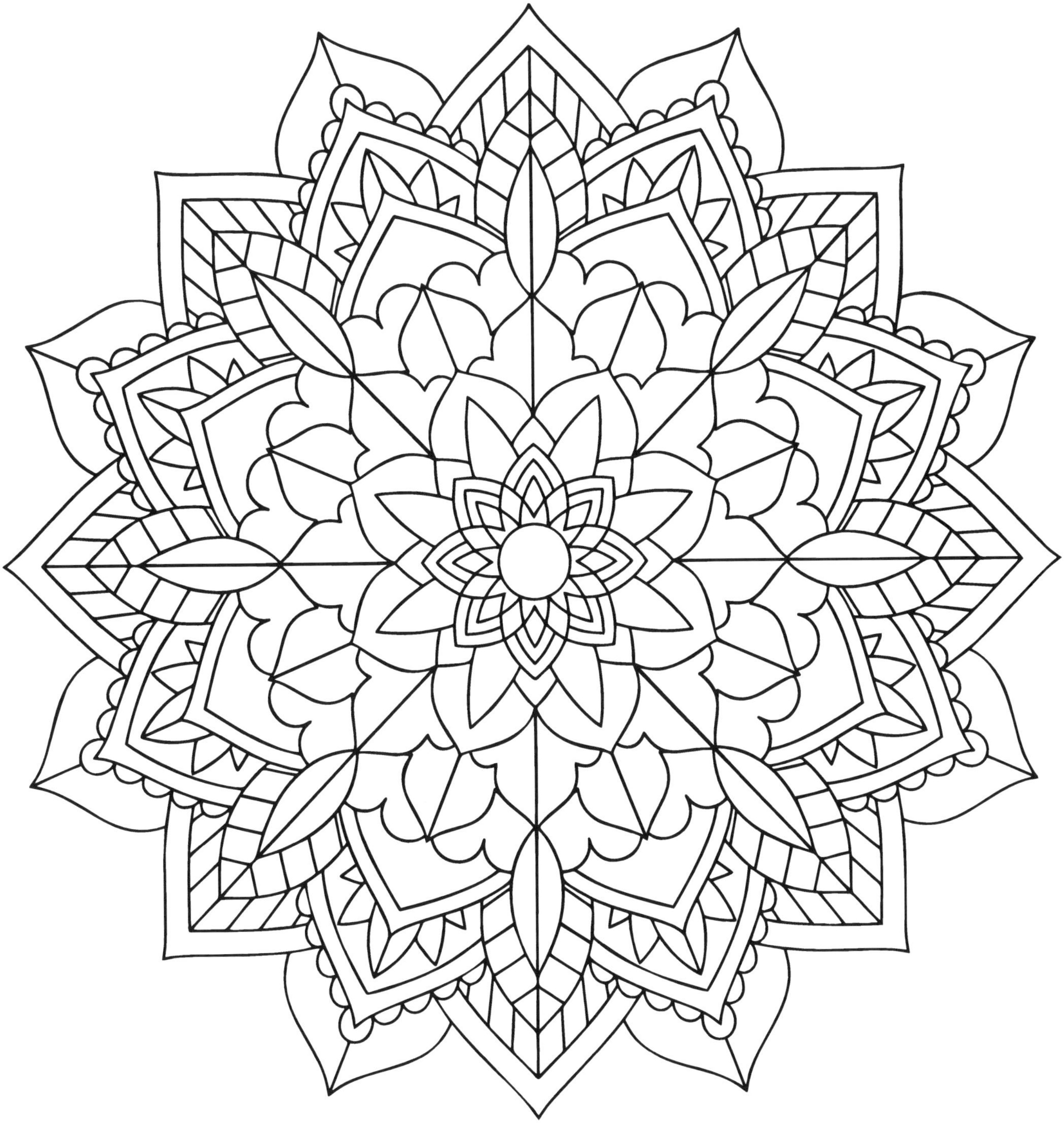

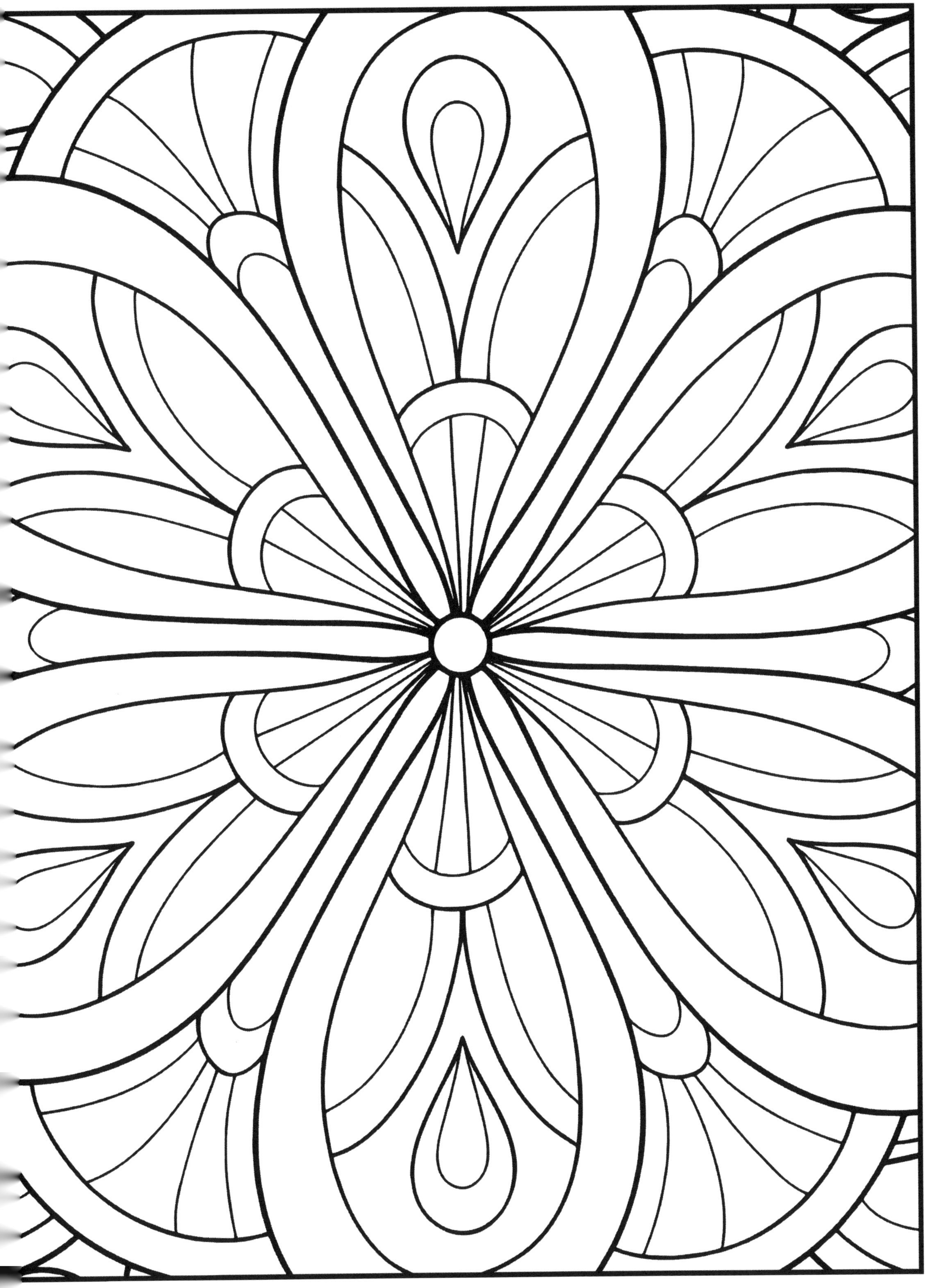

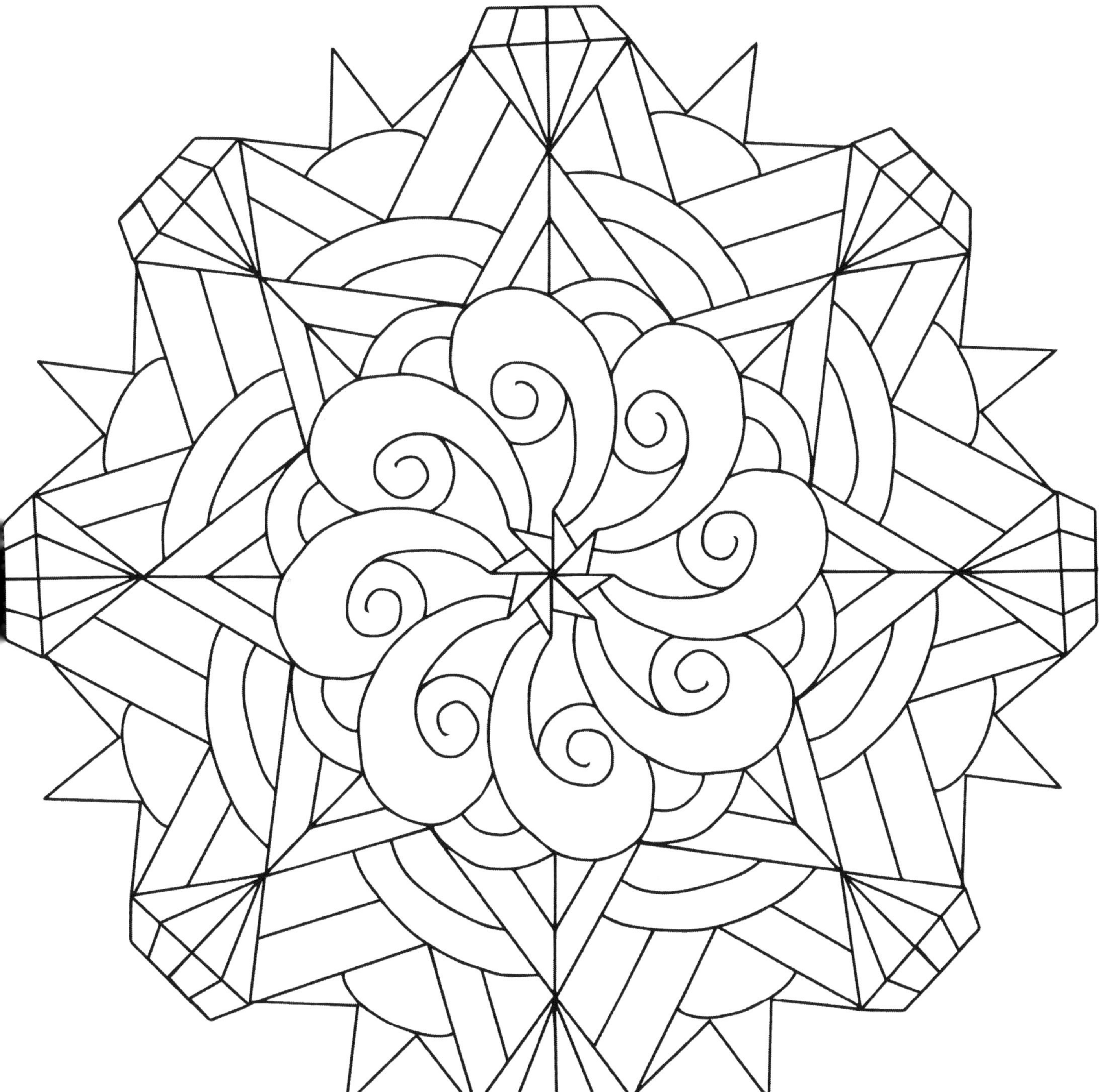

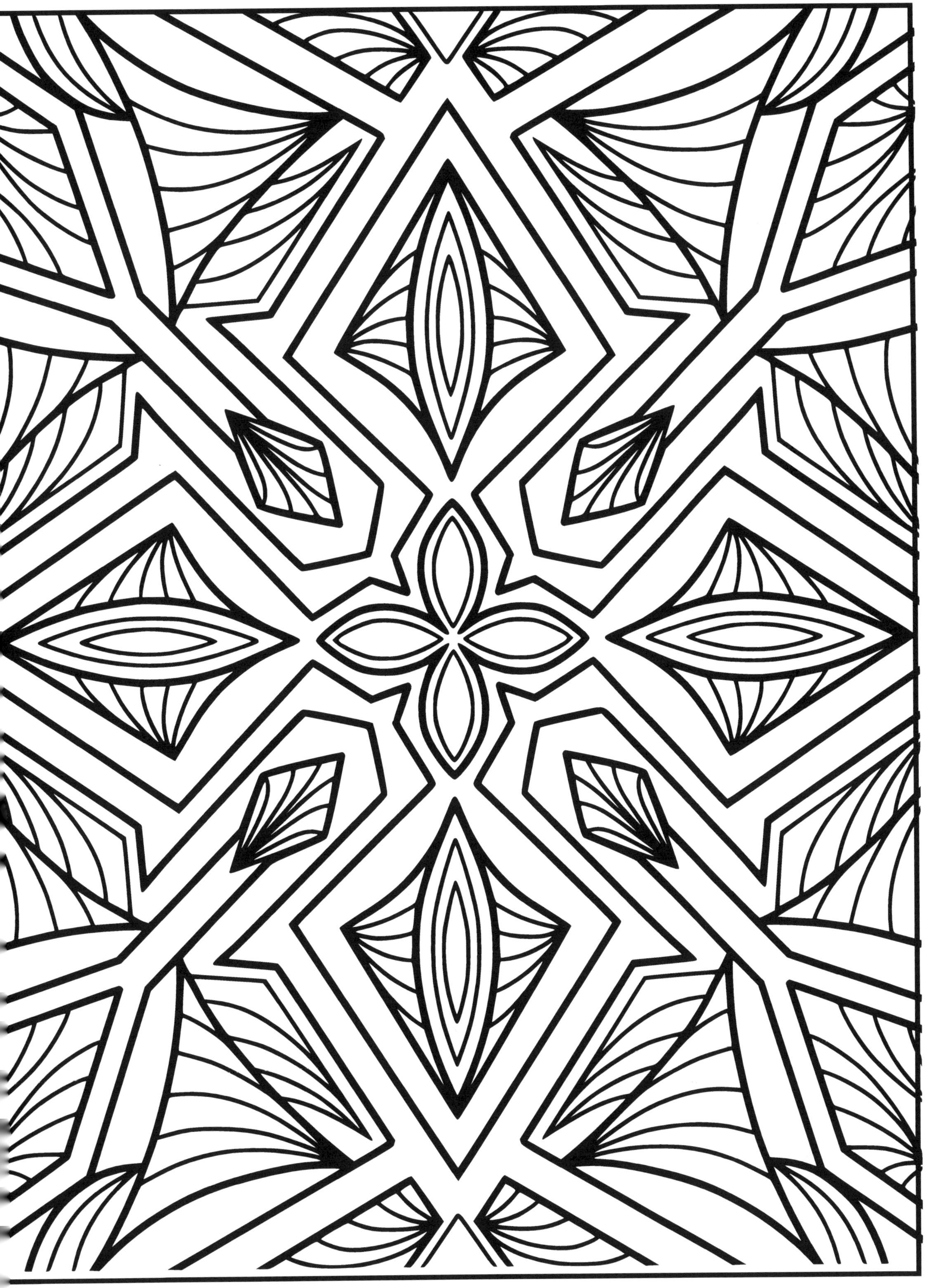

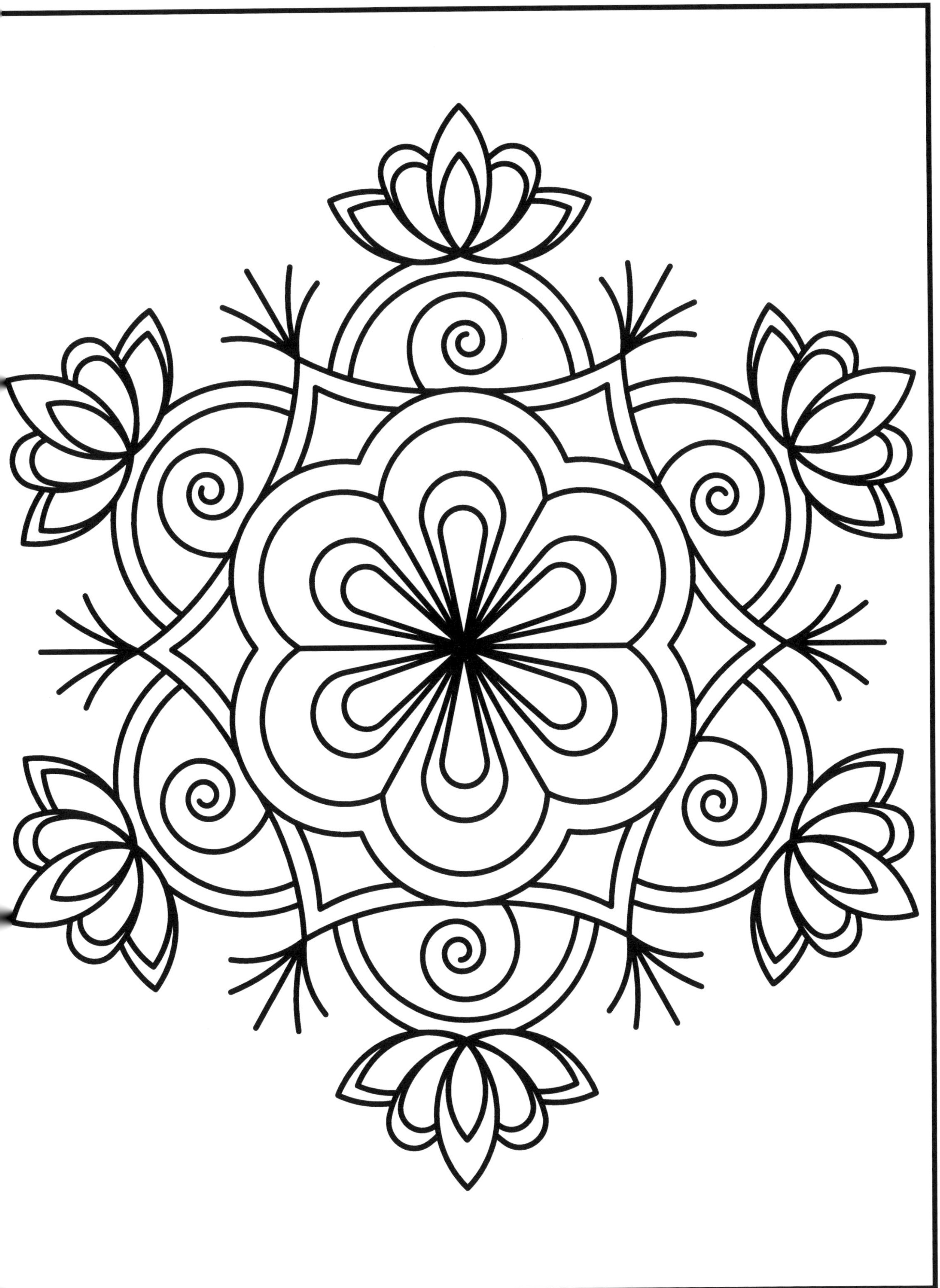

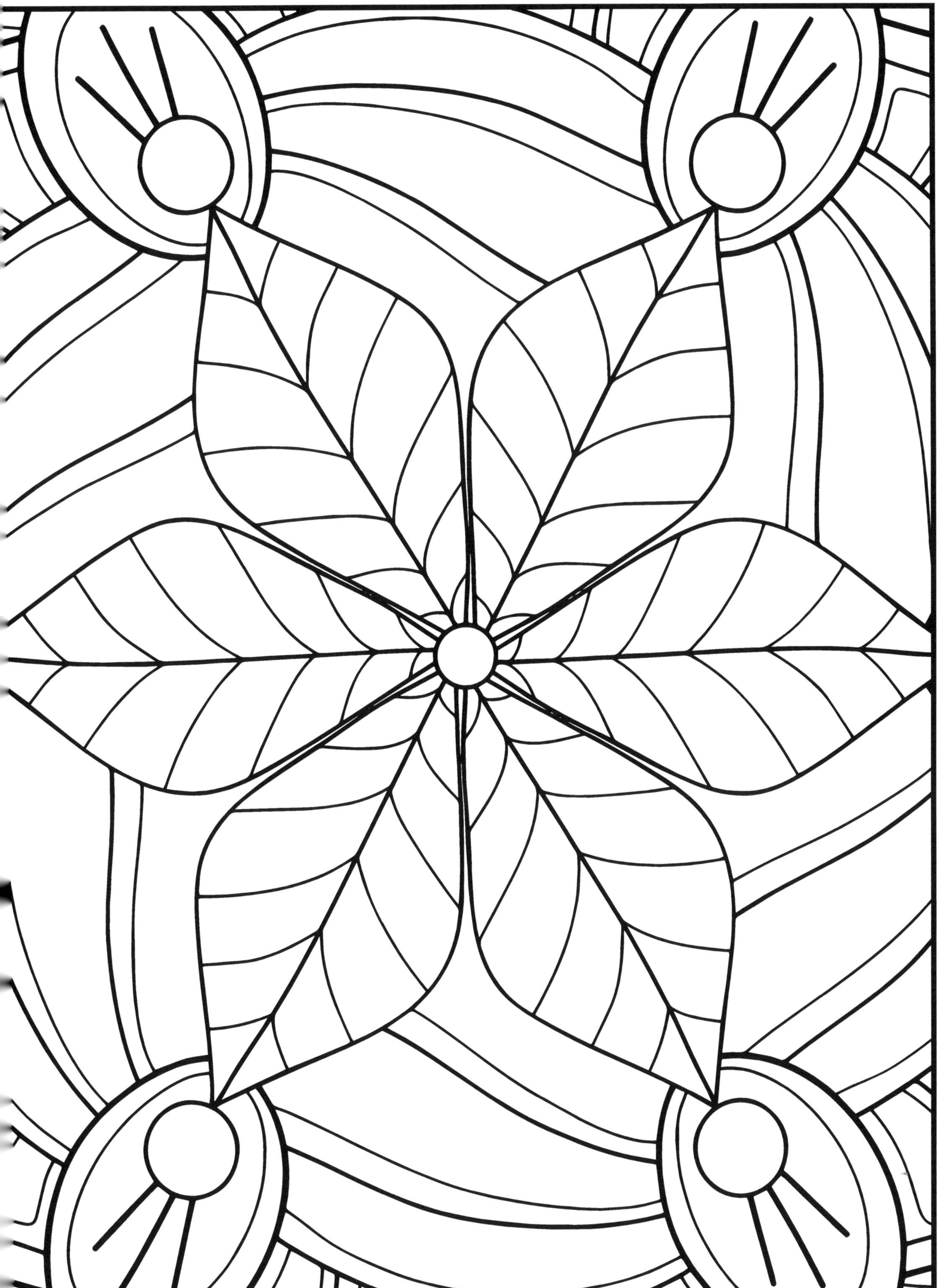

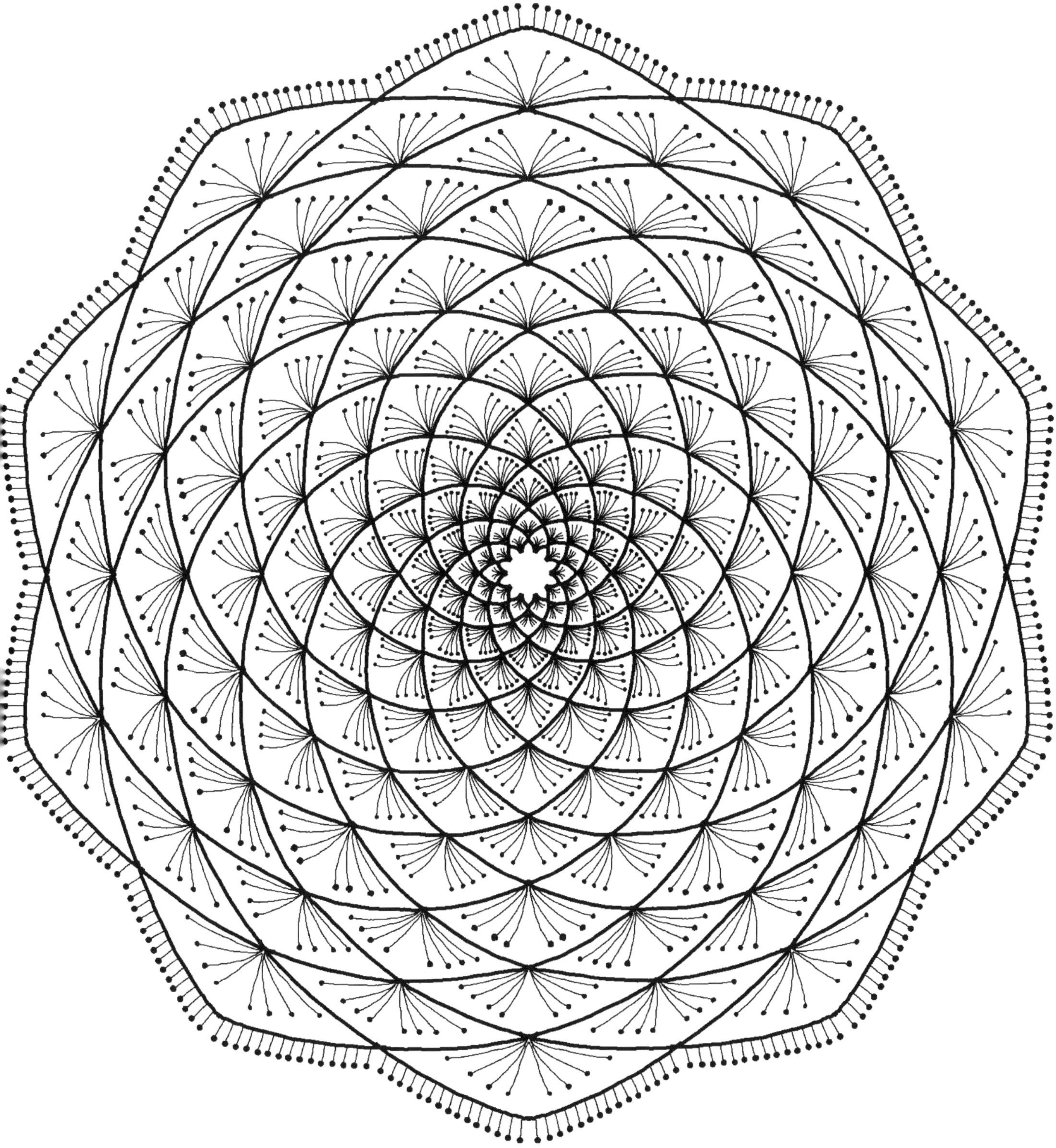

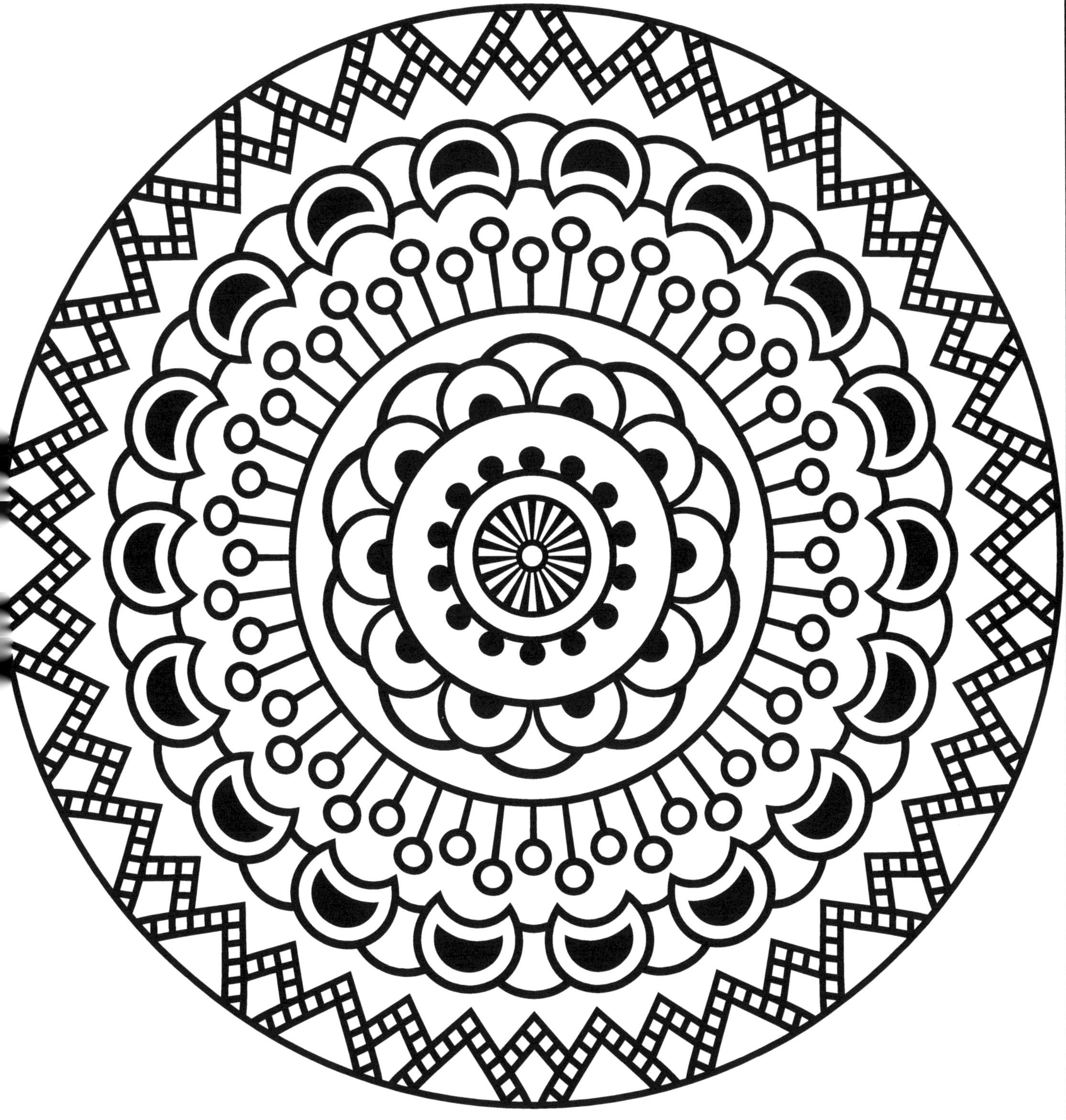

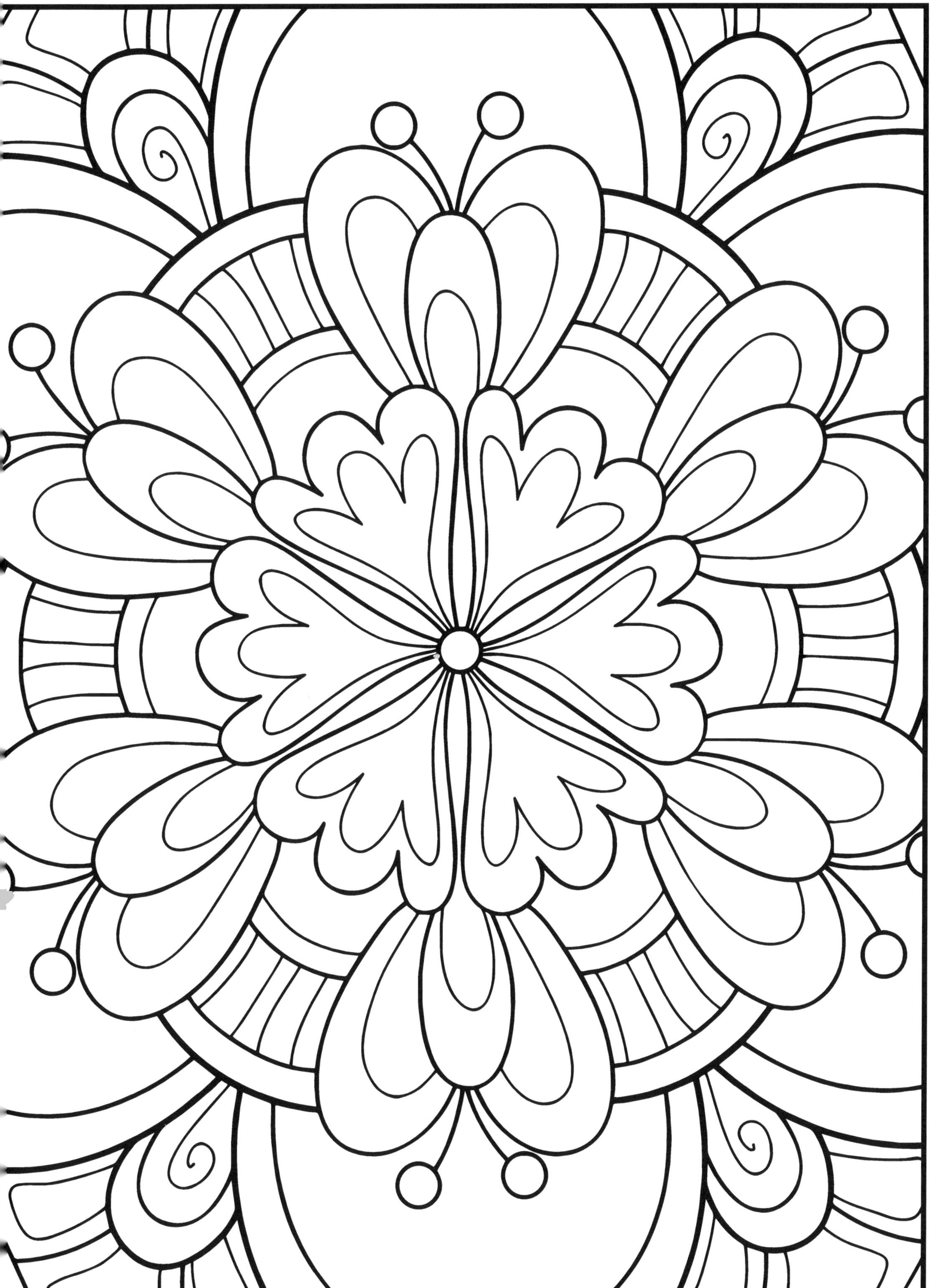

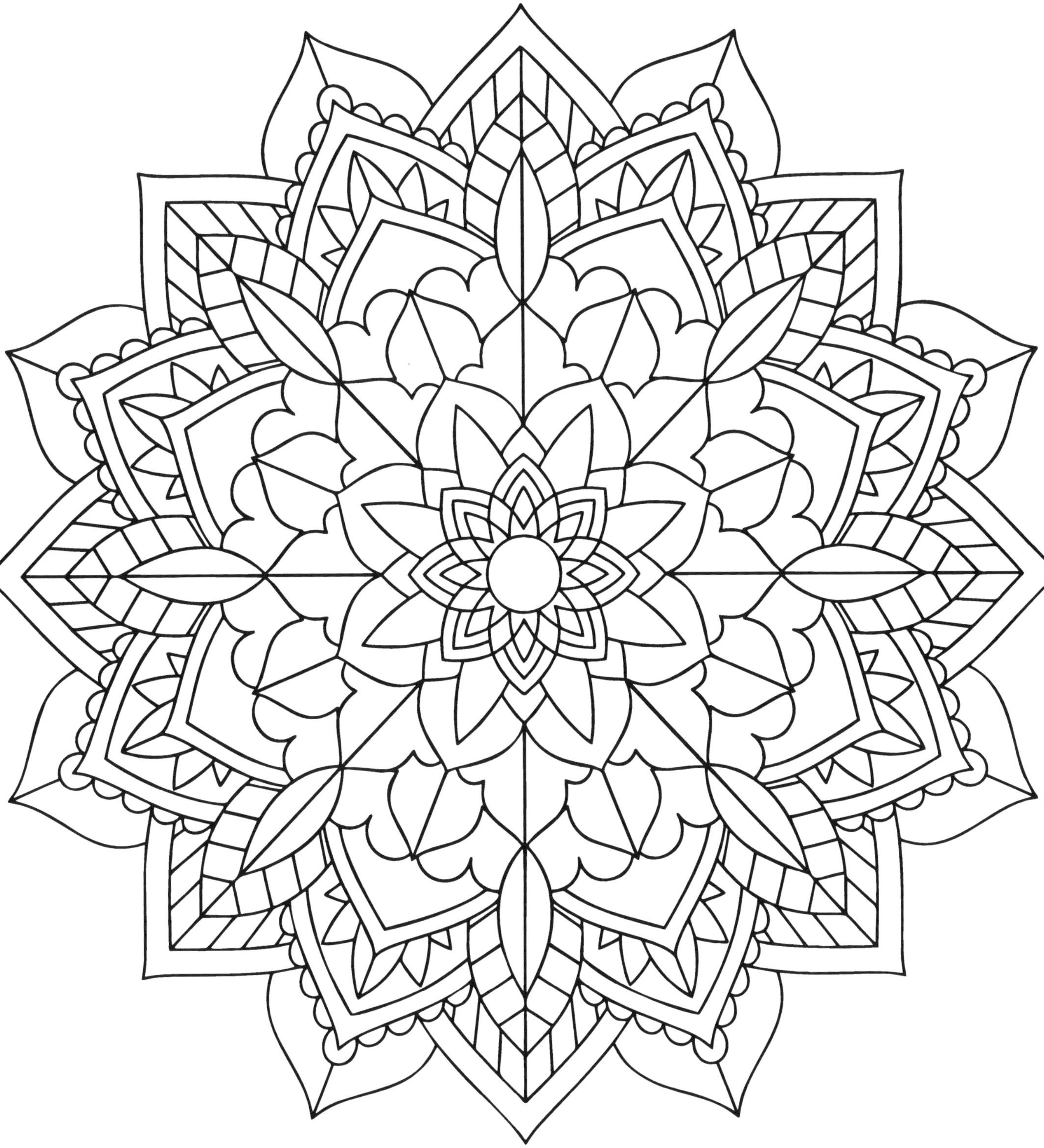

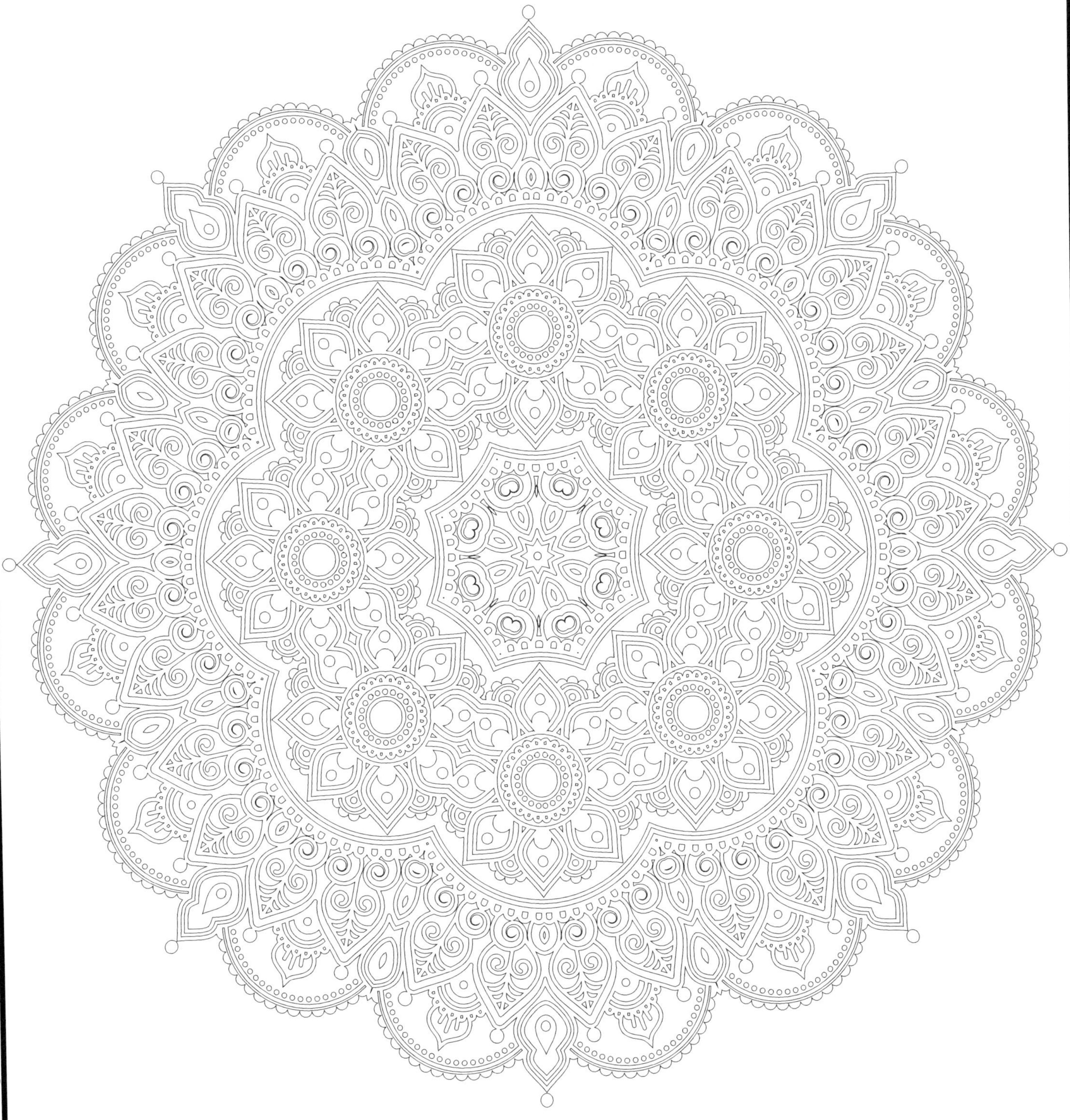

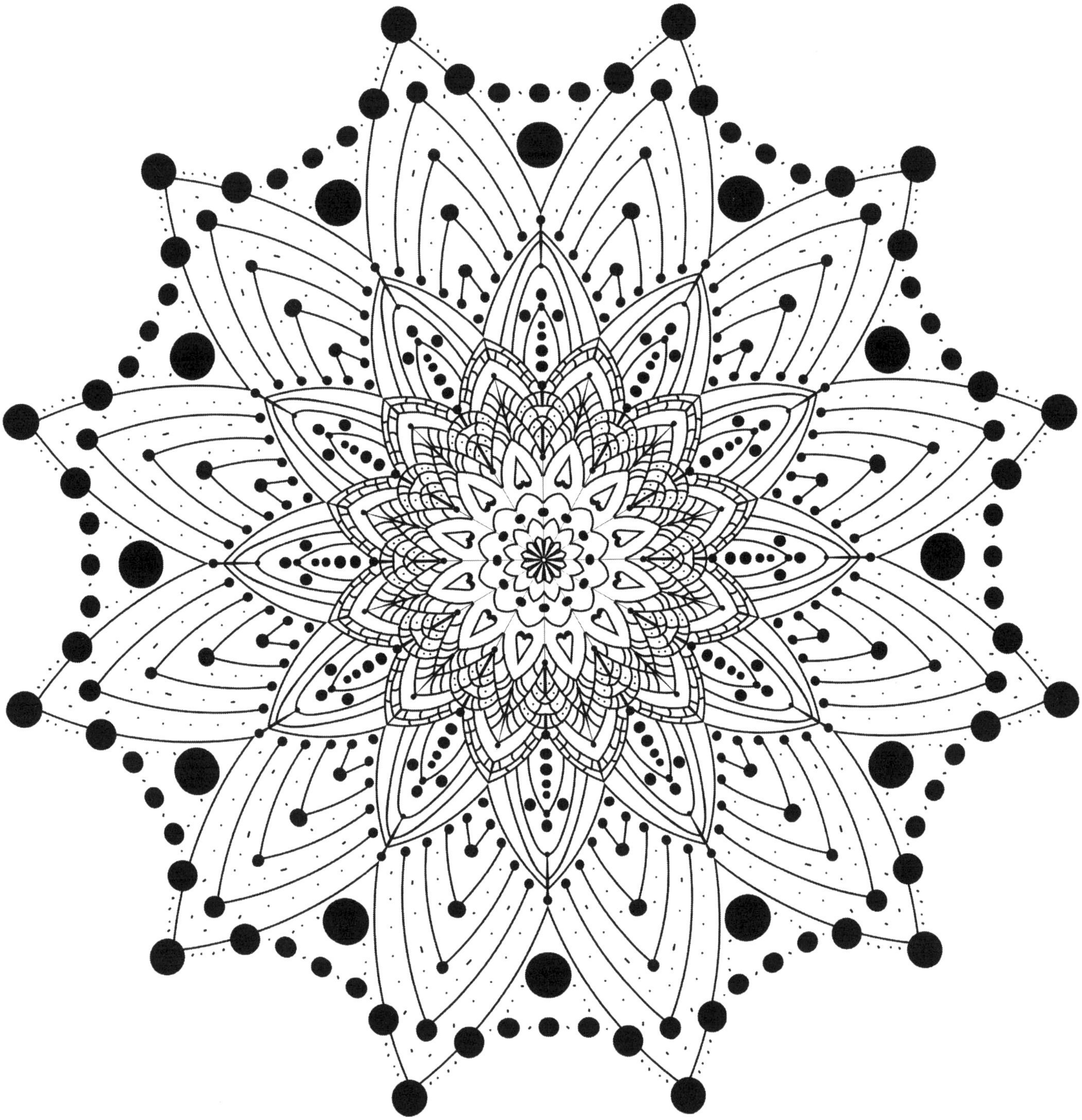

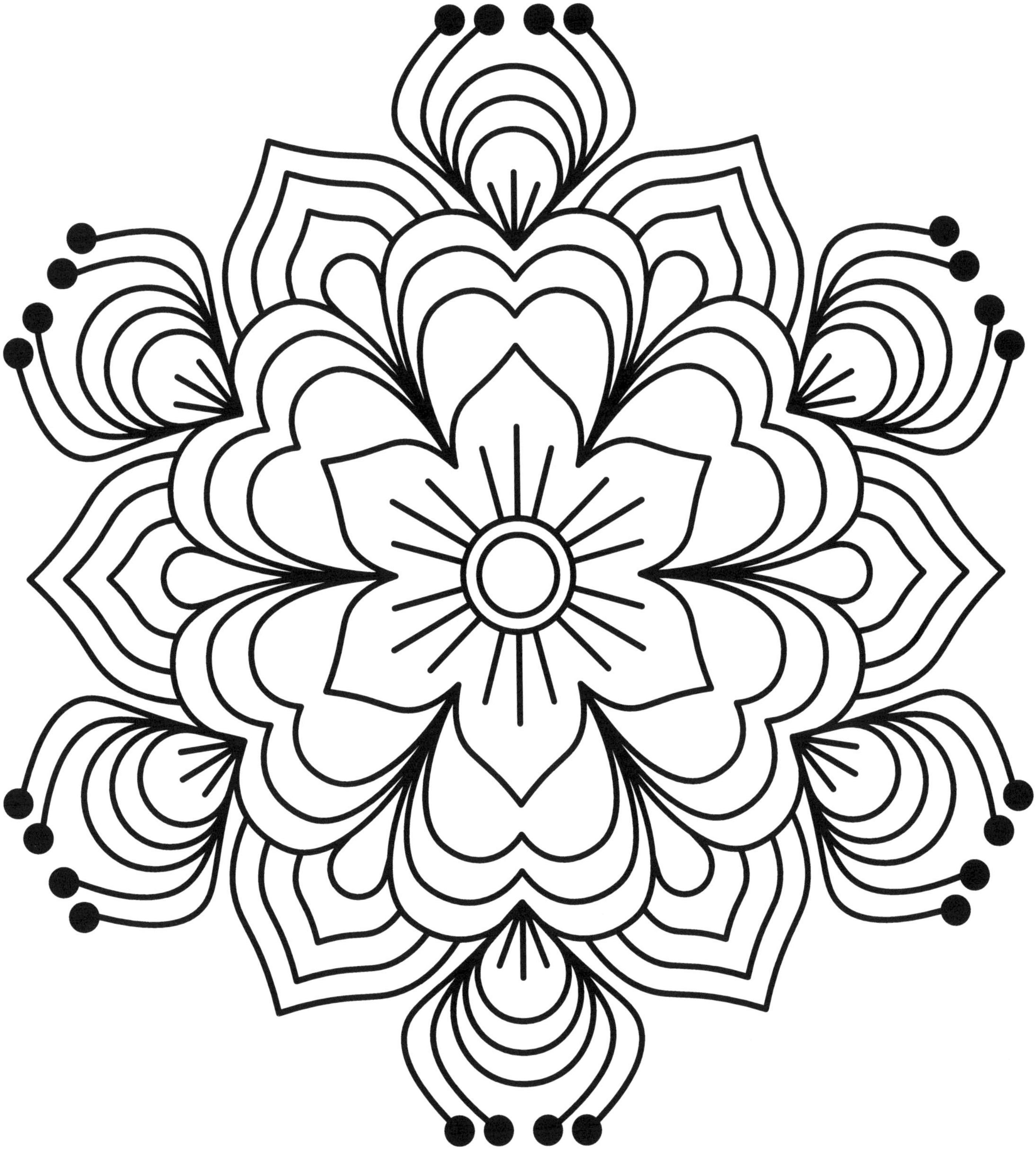

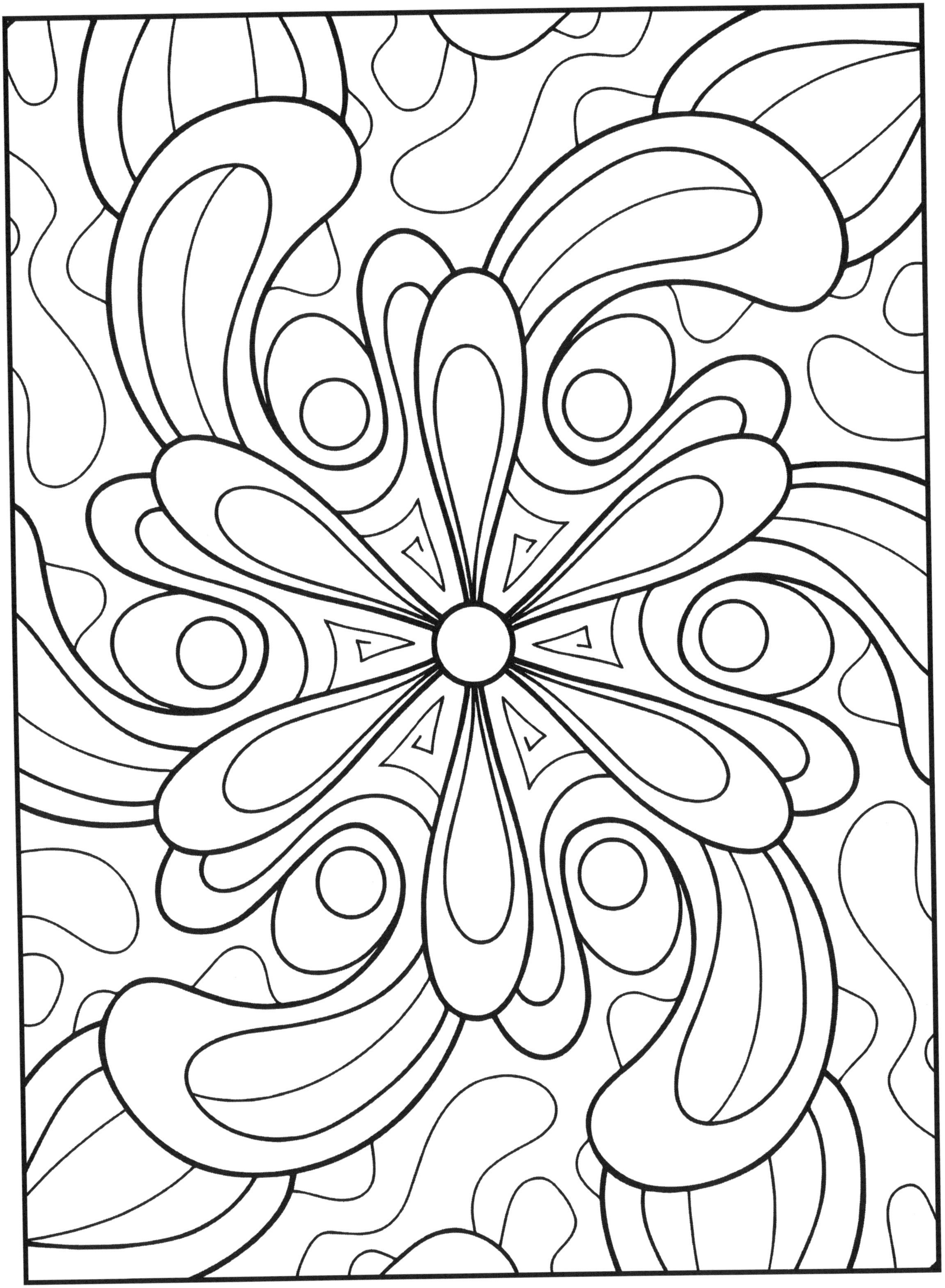

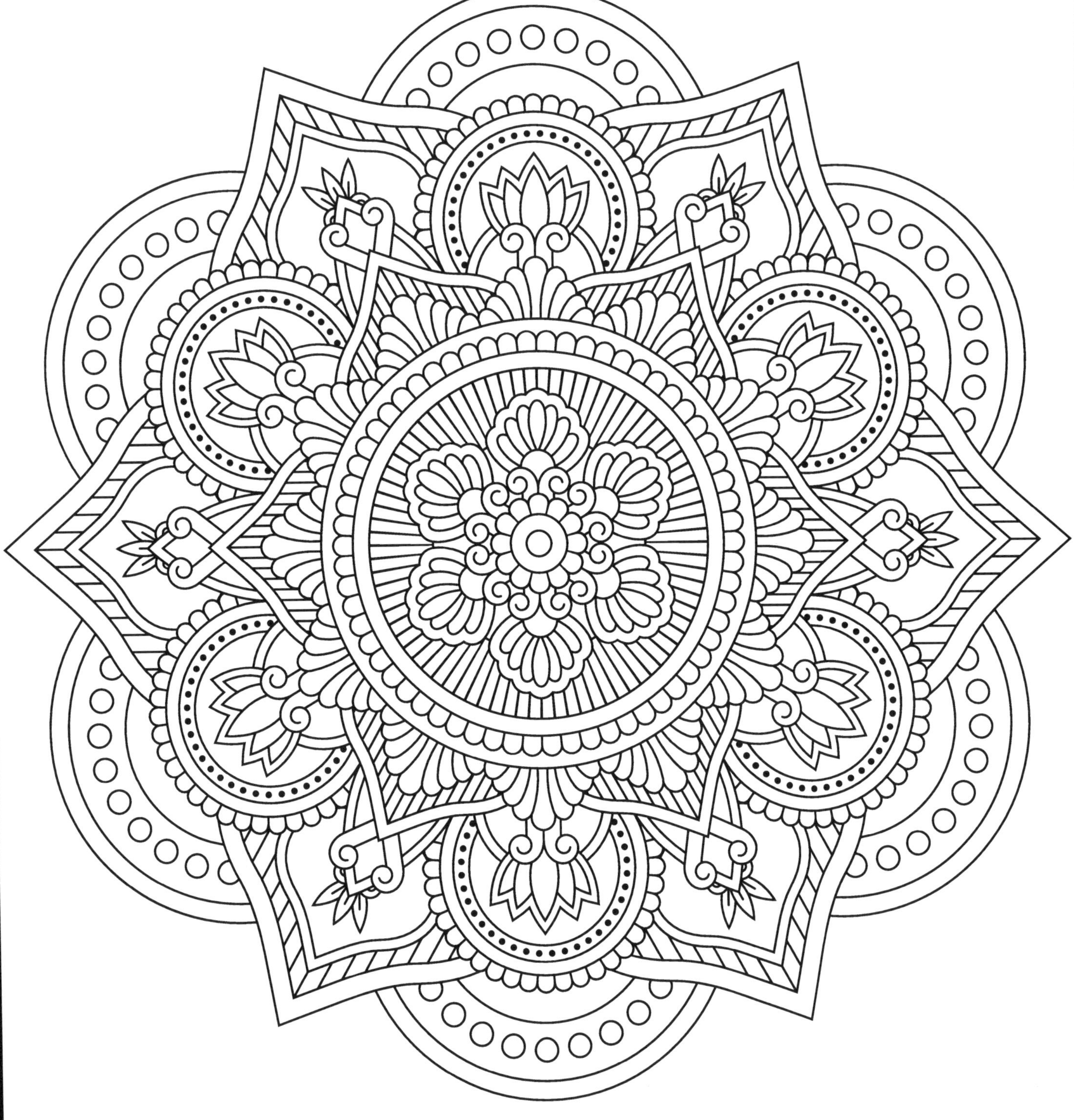

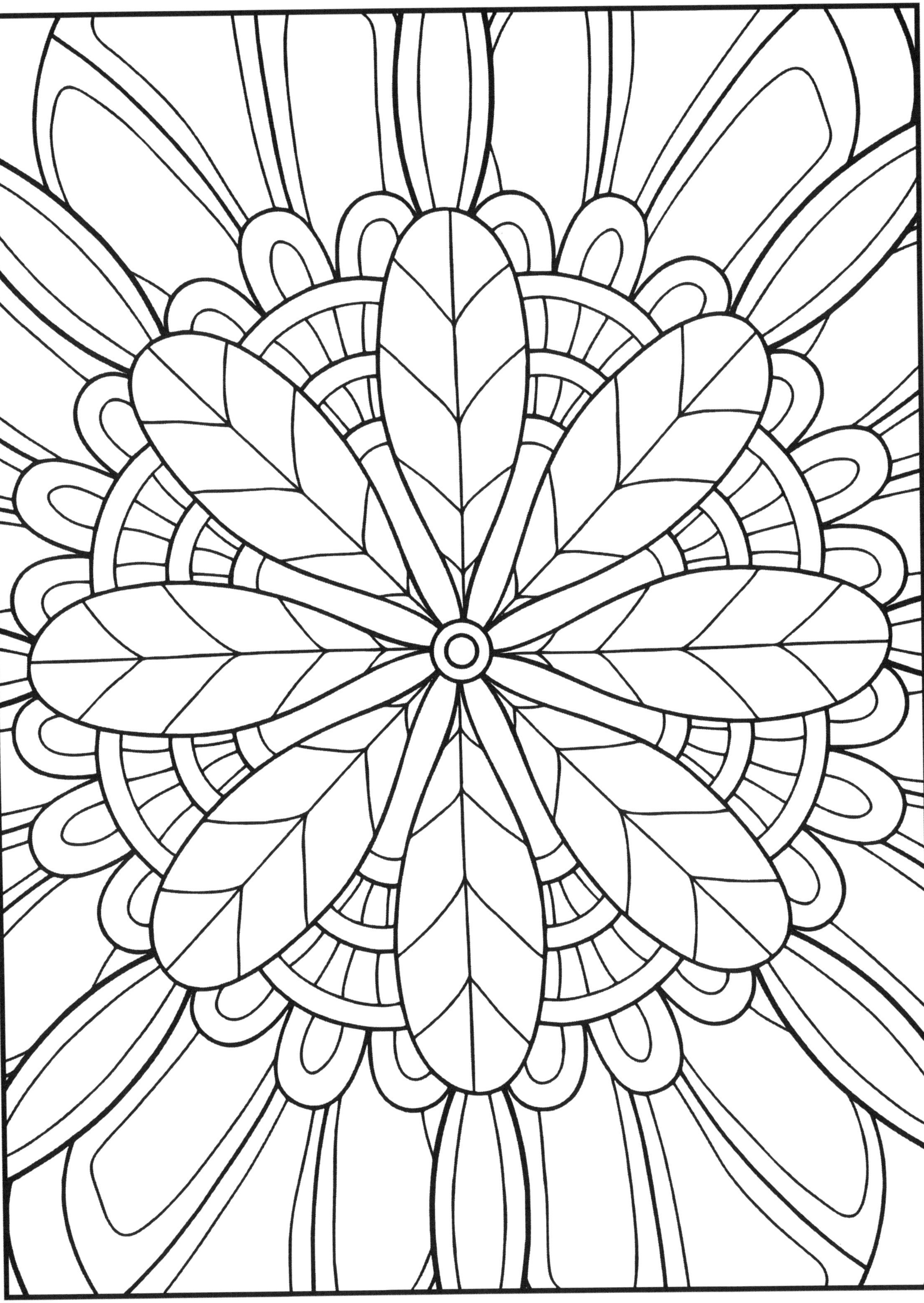

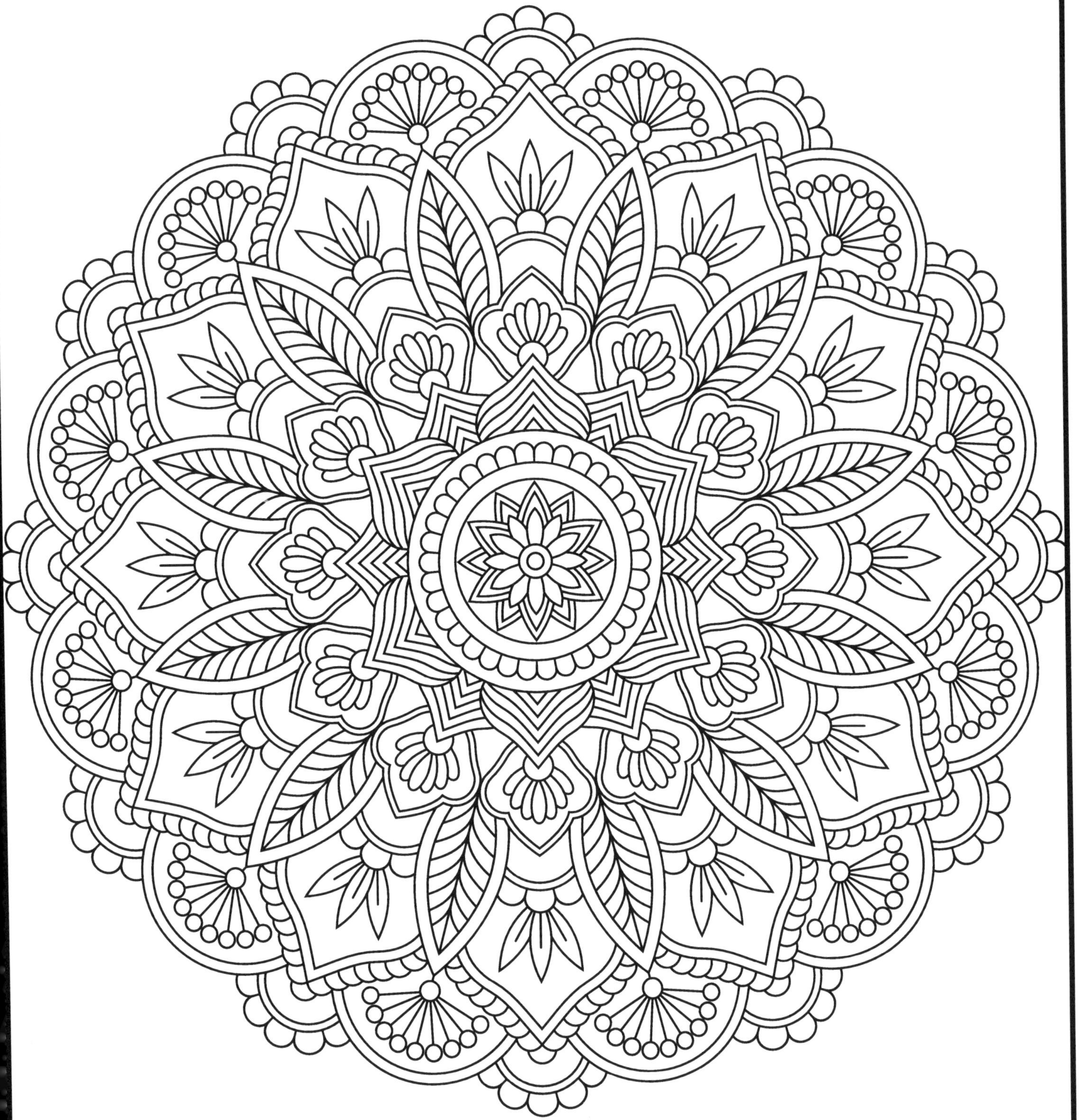

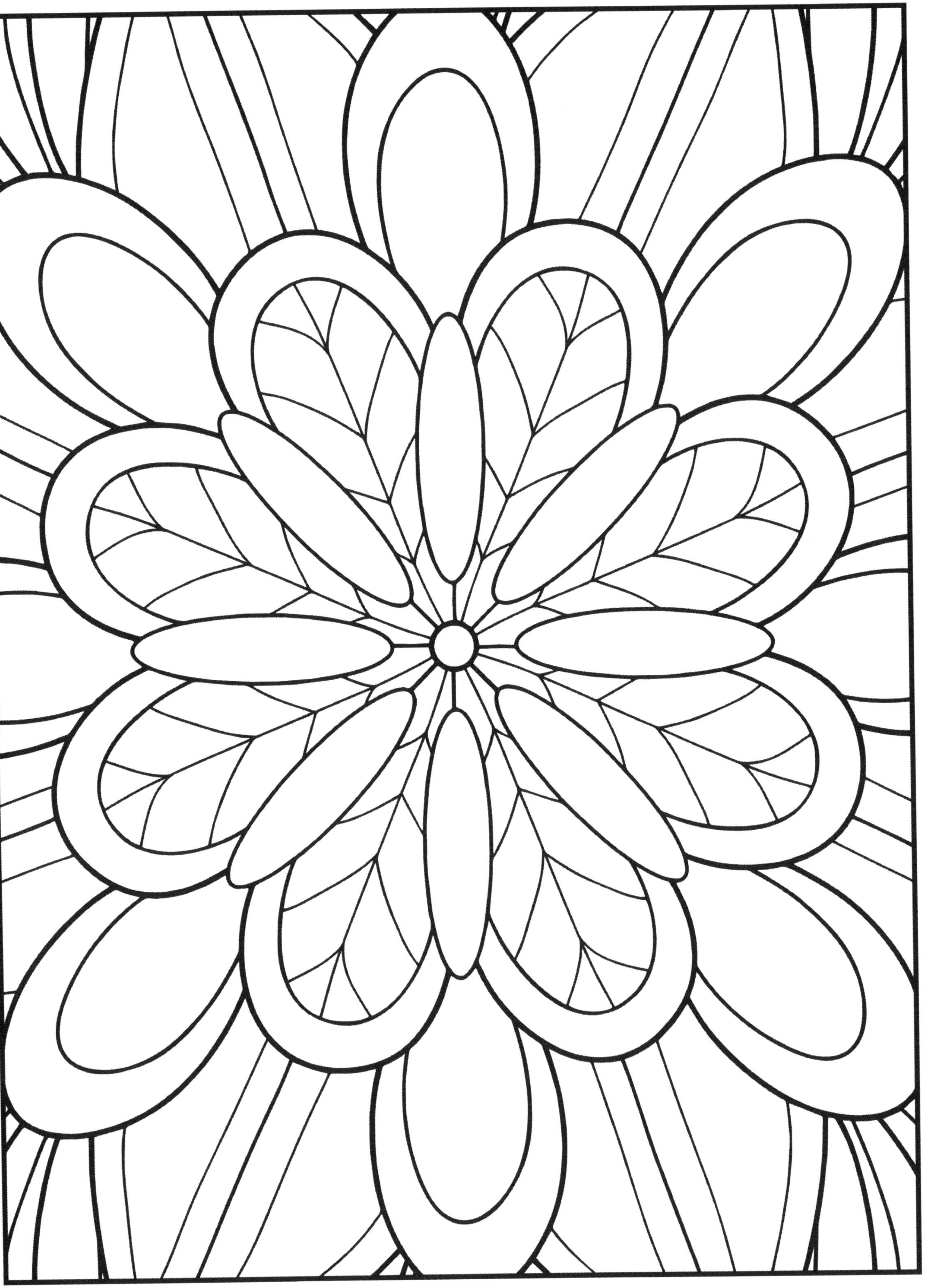

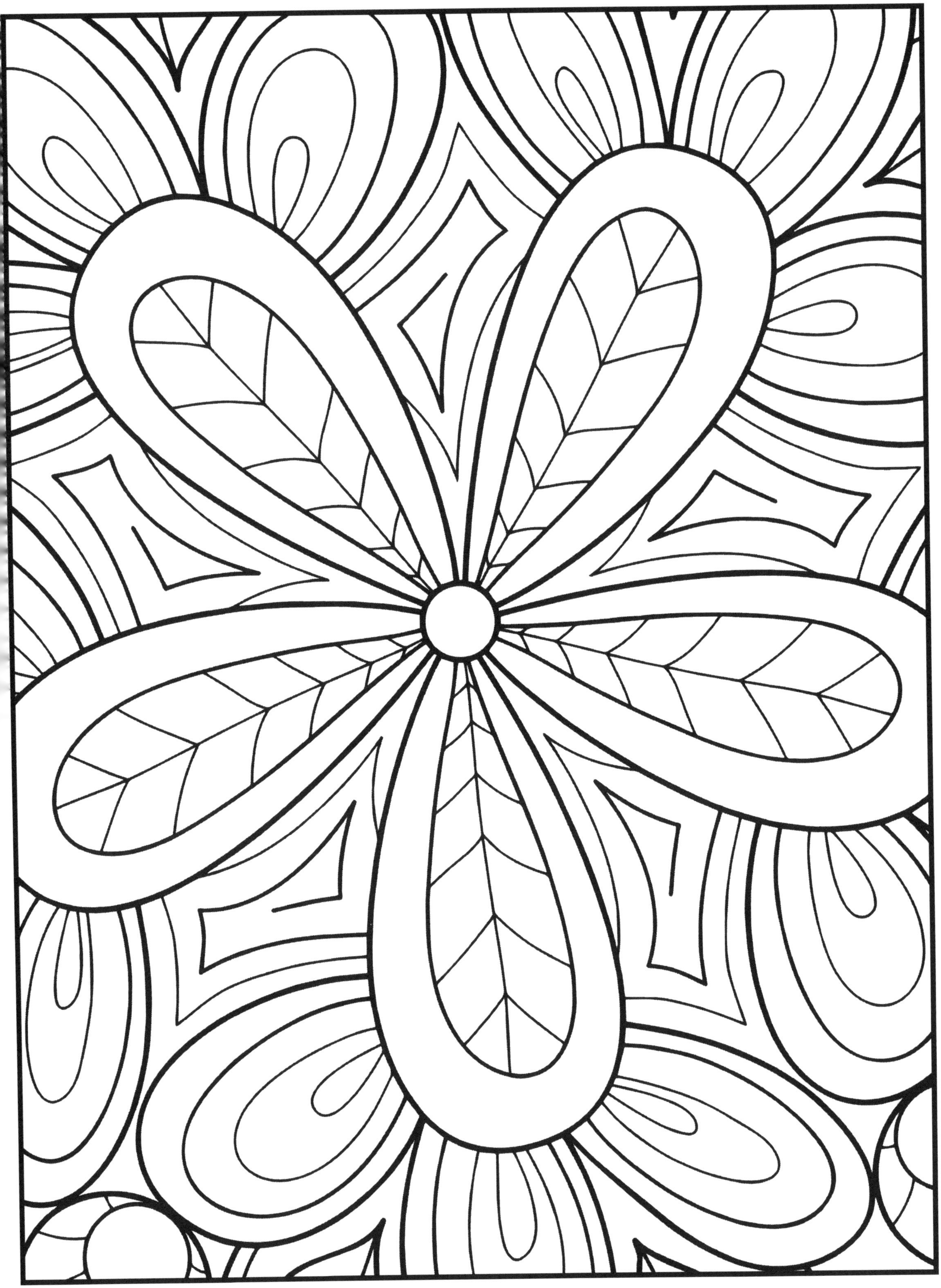

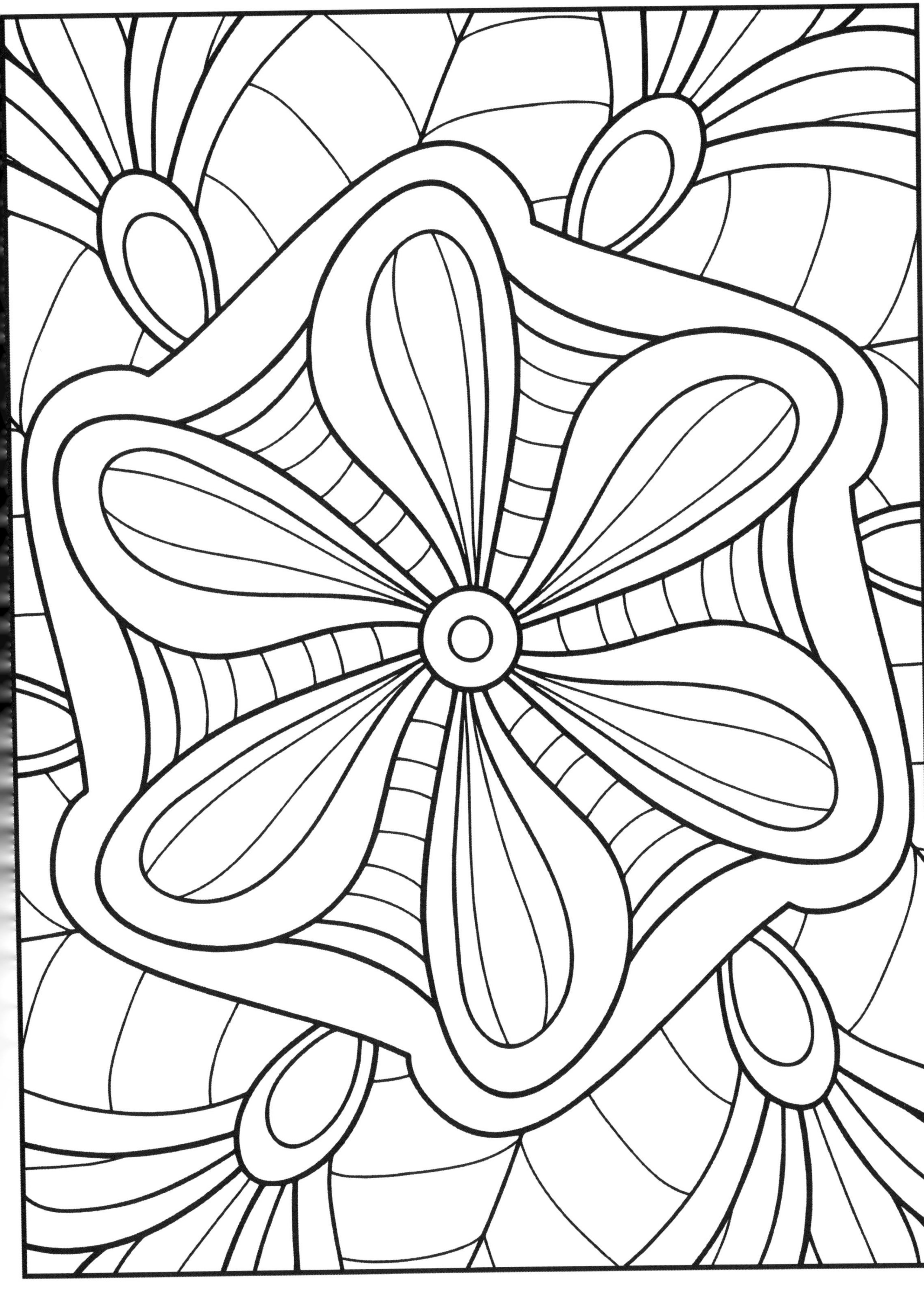

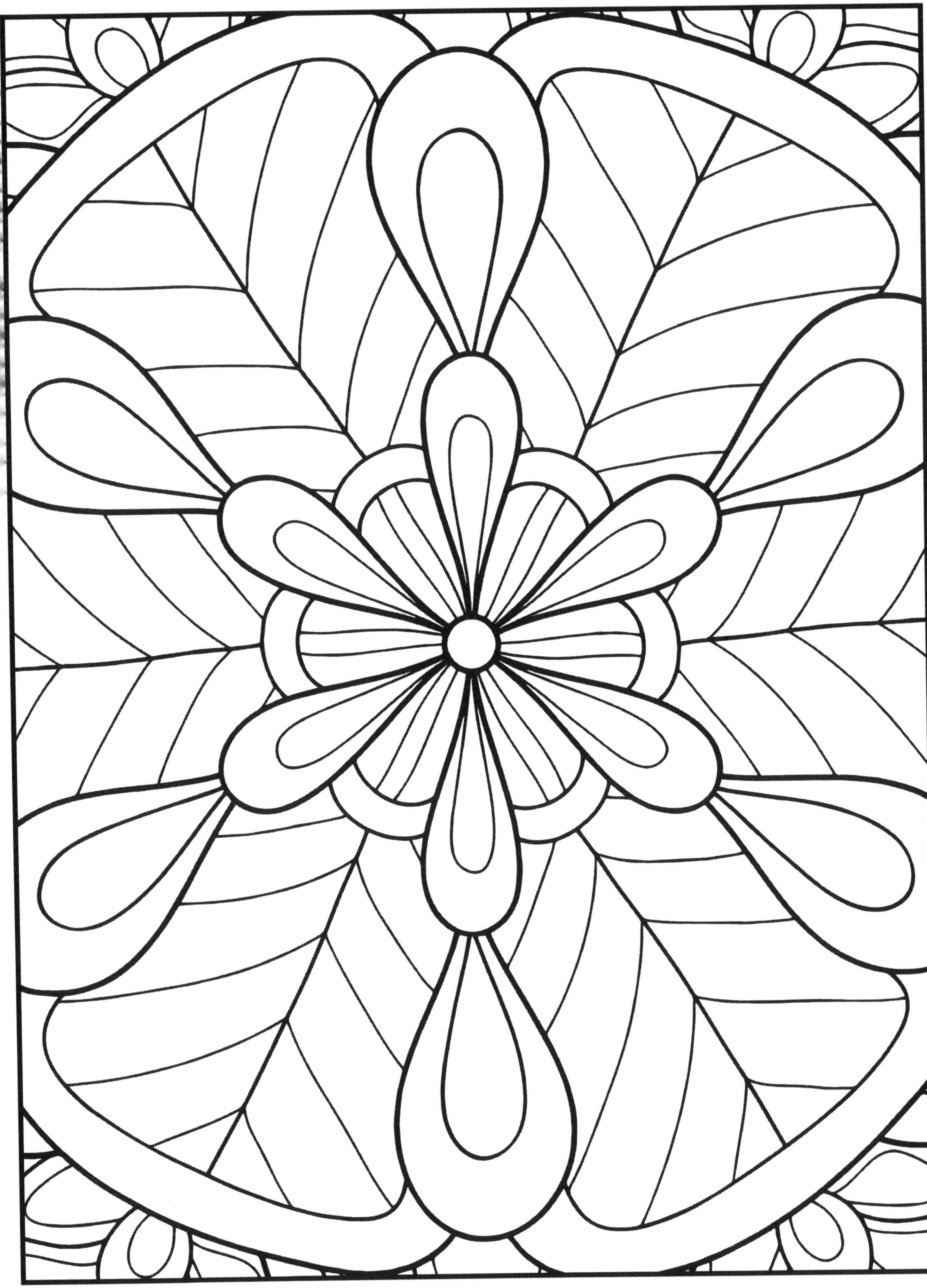

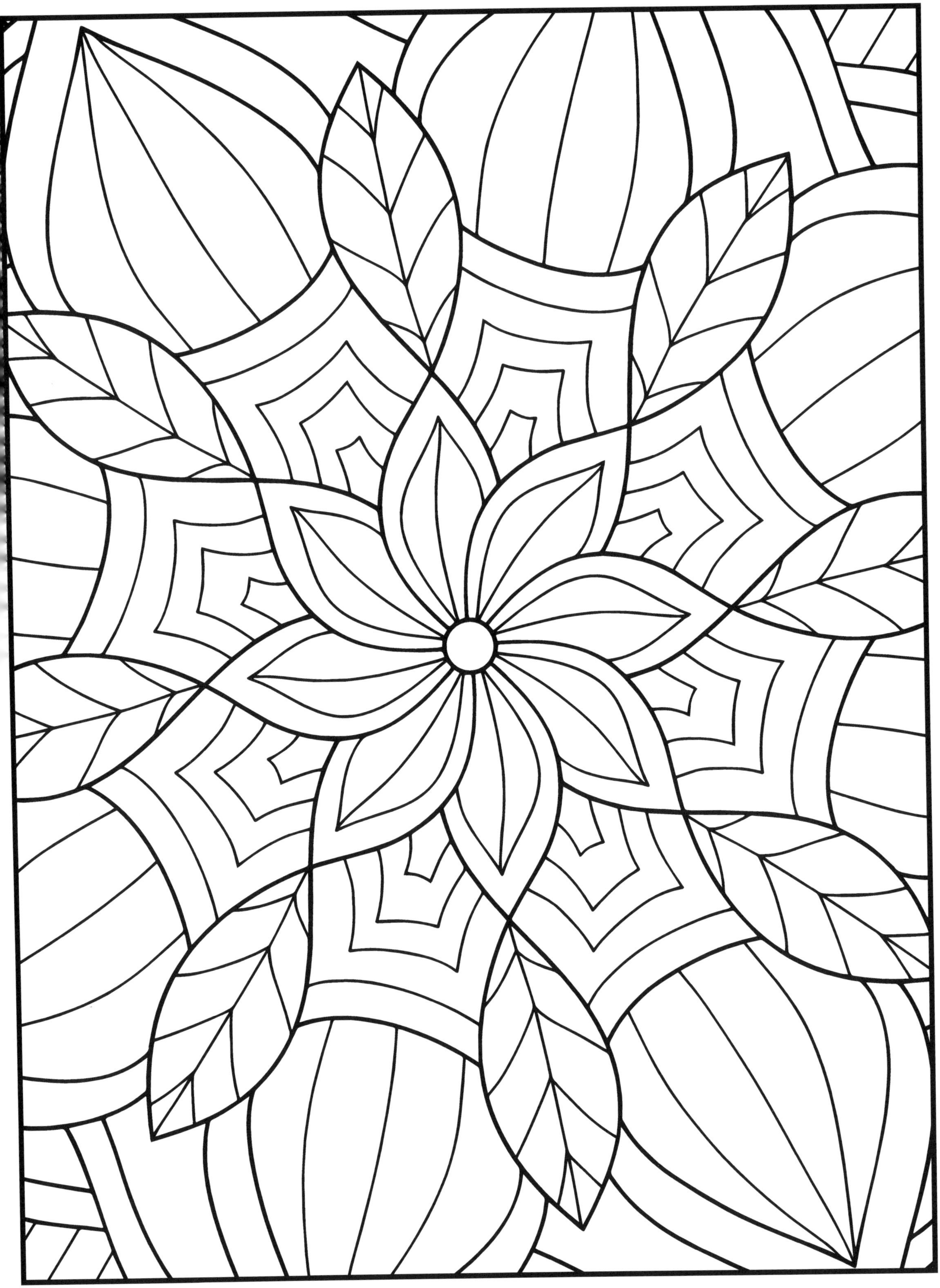

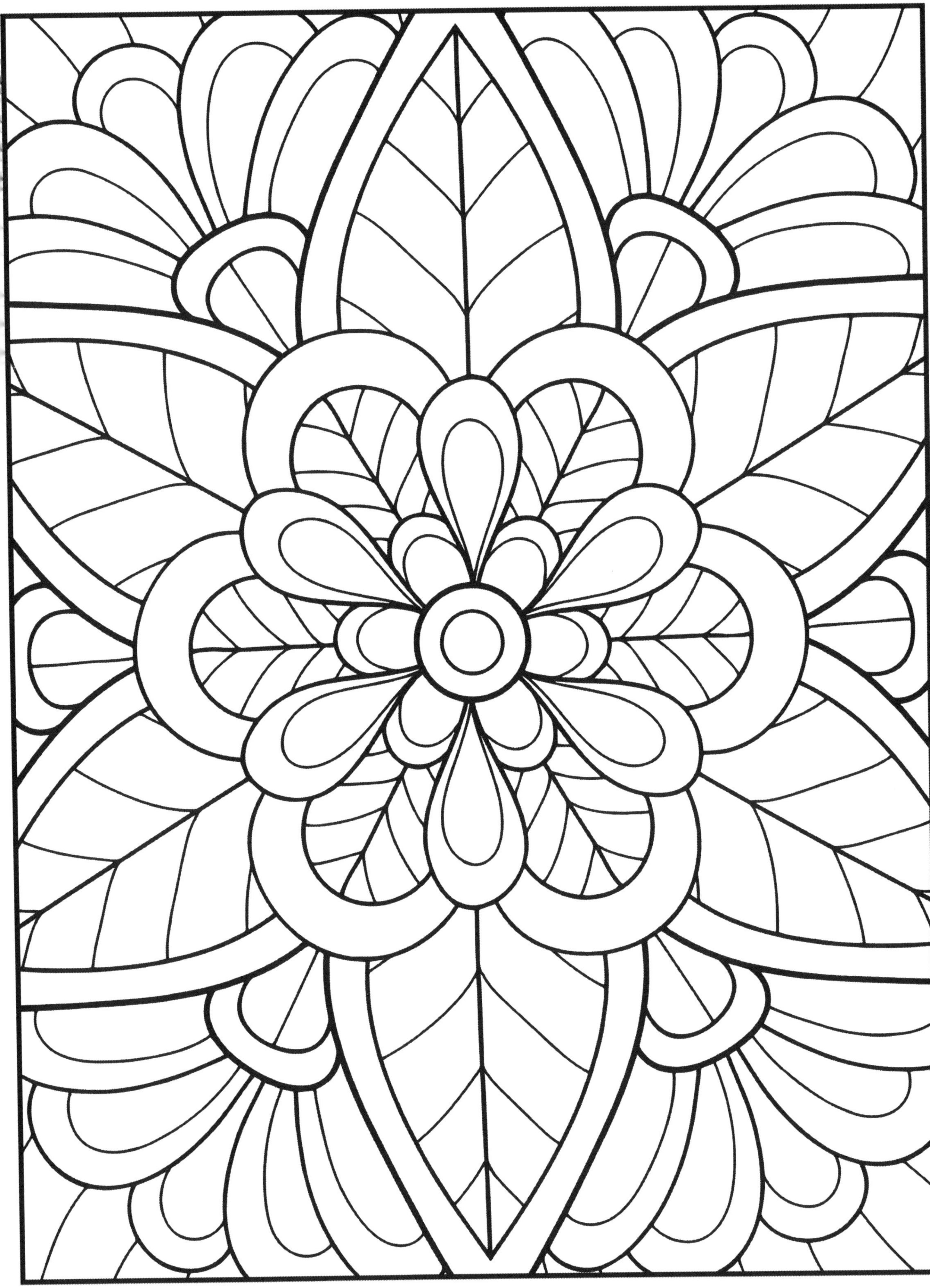

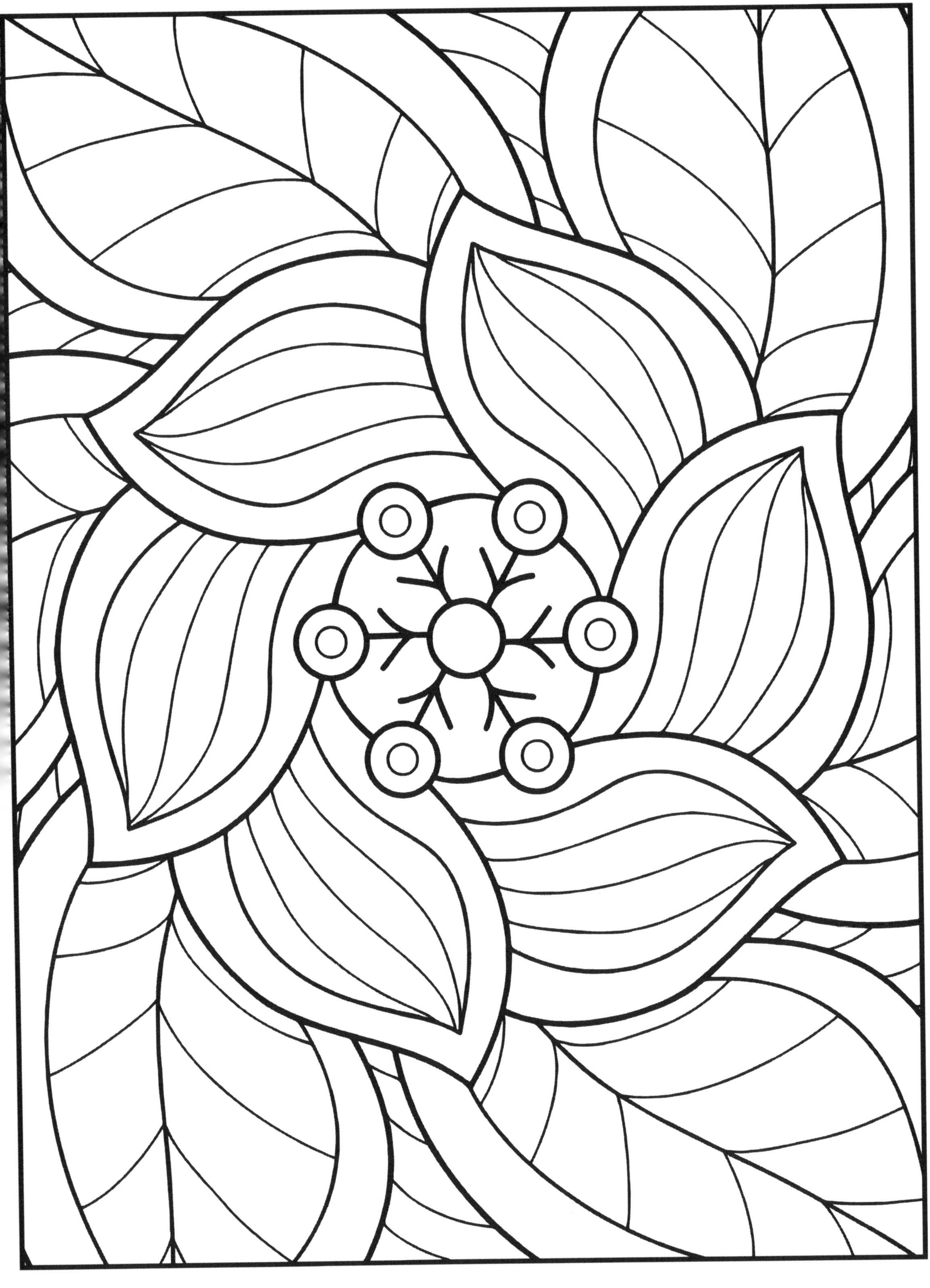

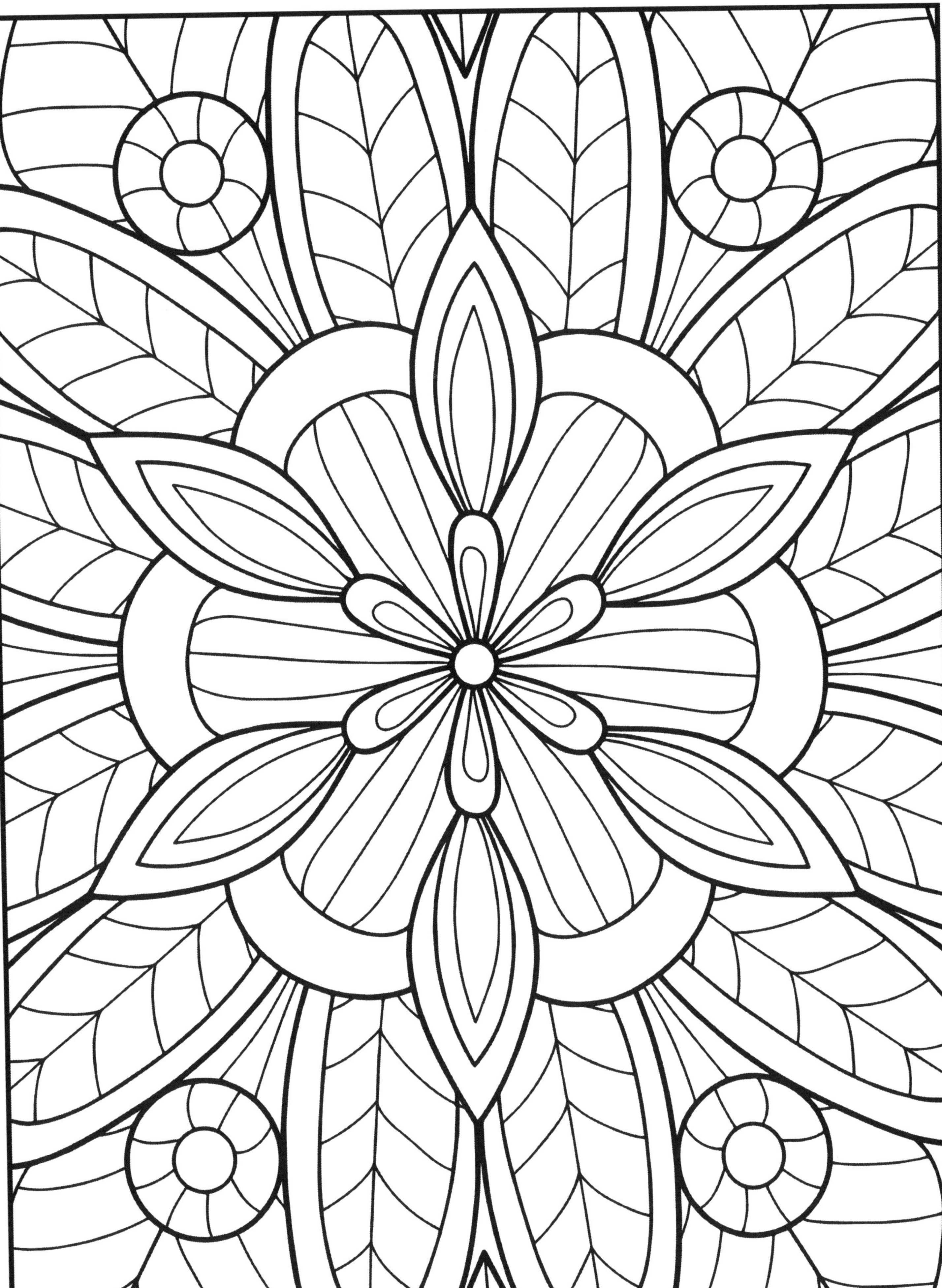

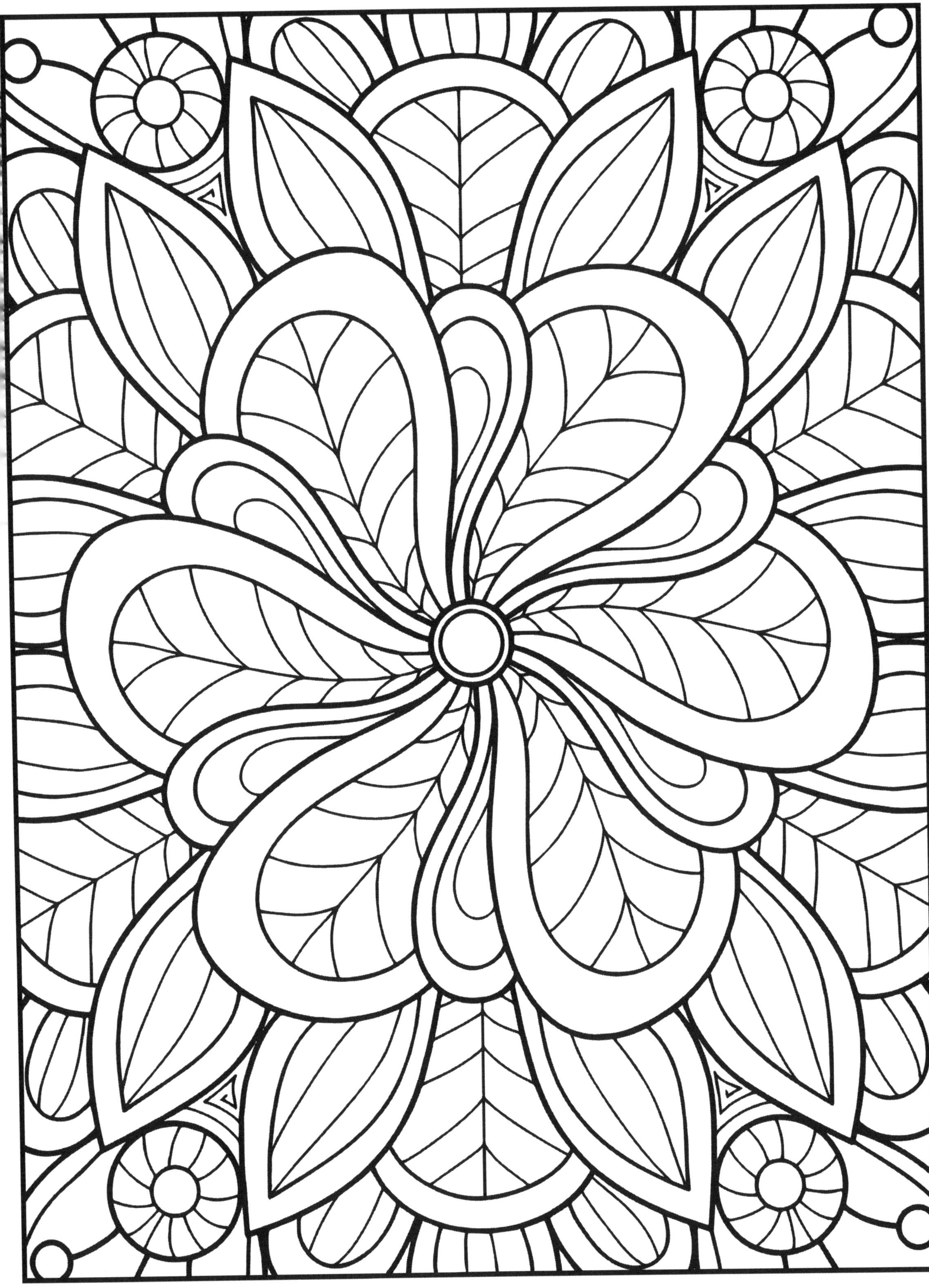

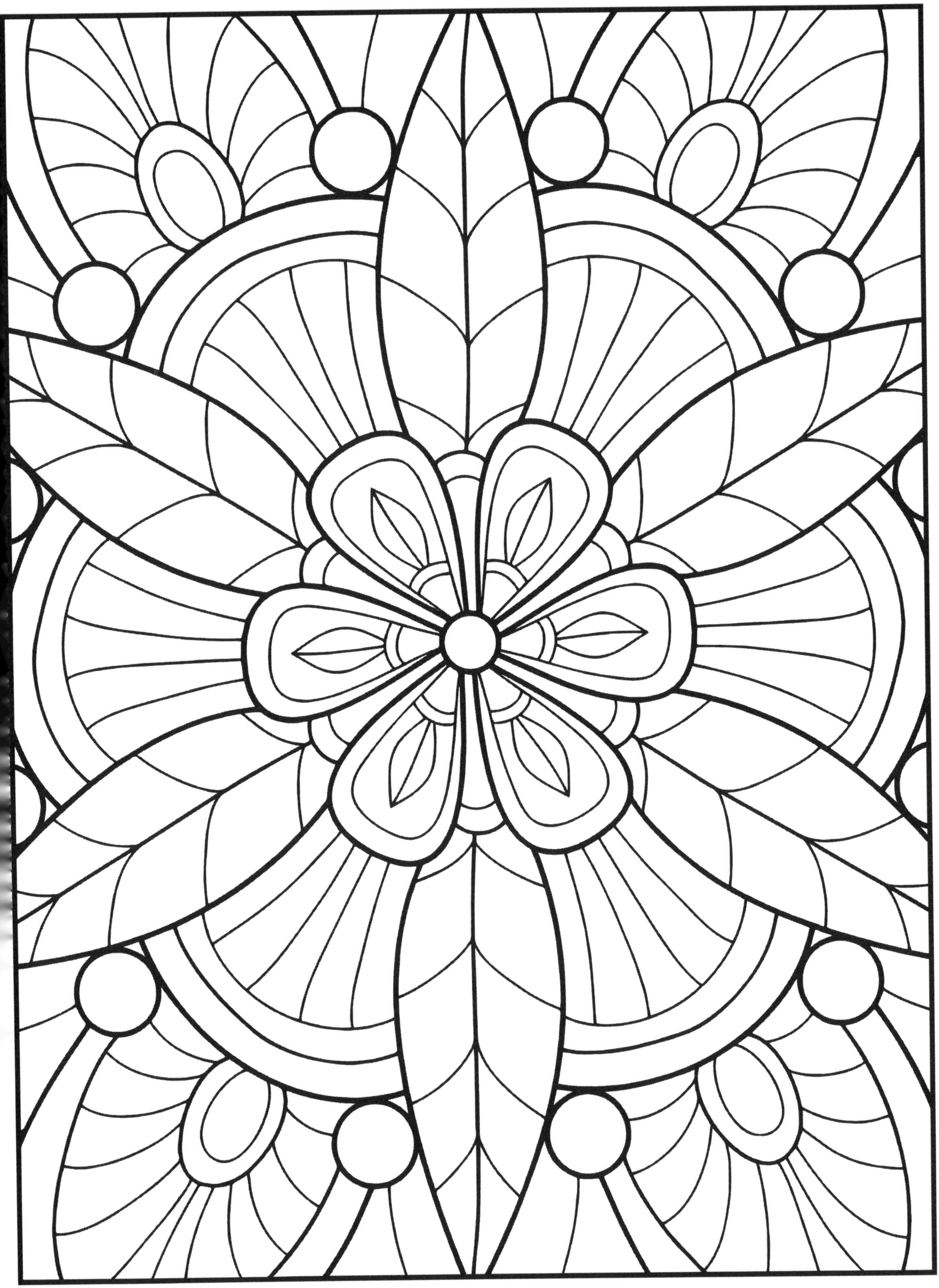

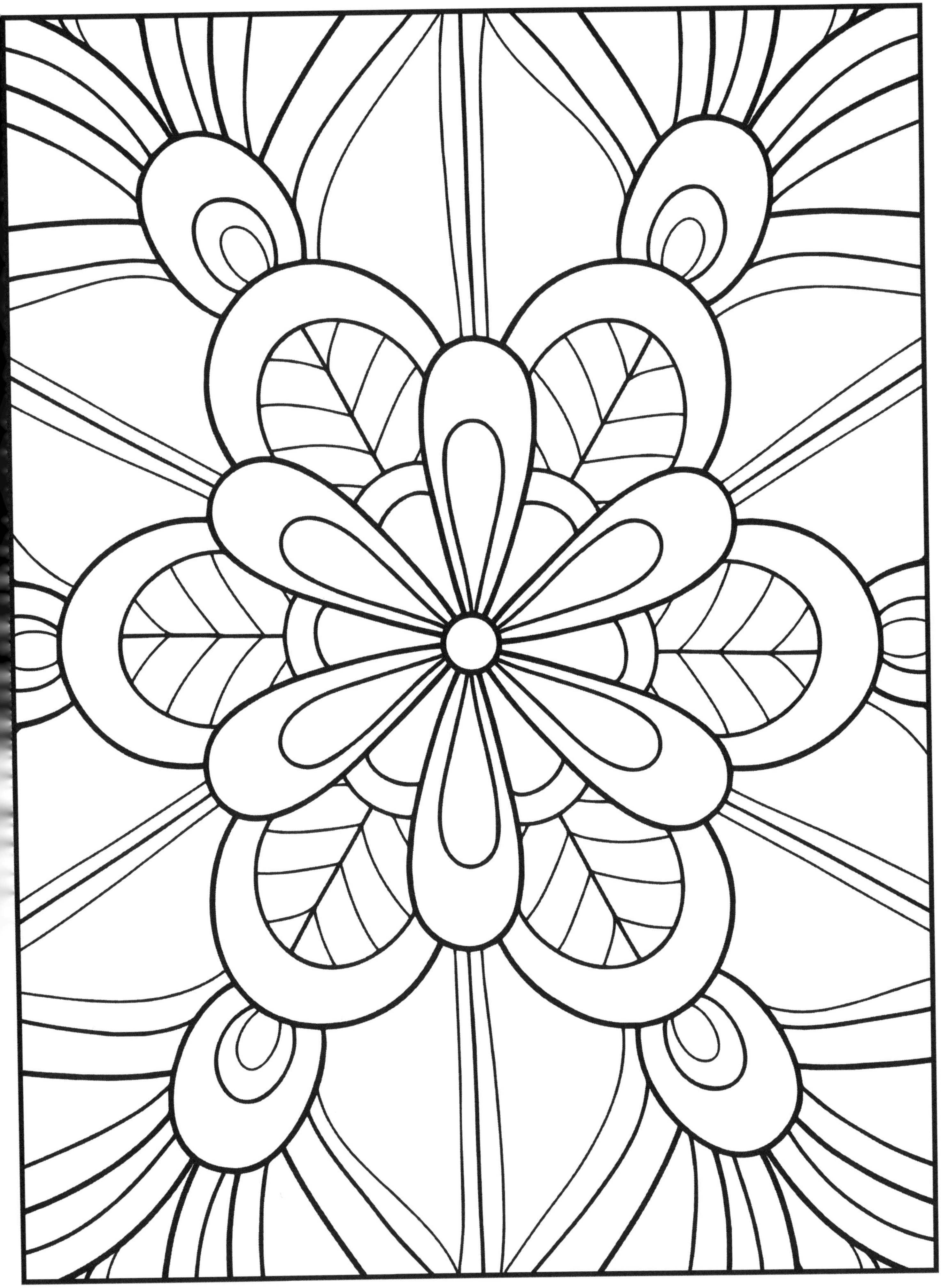

Made in the USA
Columbia, SC
18 December 2024

49880357R00050